# No Time

# The Unofficial Retrospective

John Fox

# Contents

# CHAPTER ONE - THE WAITING GAME AGAIN

Thanks to circumstances beyond the control of anyone, No Time to Die did not make its projected early 2021 release date. The long wait continued to drag on and on but it wouldn't last forever. At some point they were going to have to bite the bullet and take a gamble on releasing No Time to Die in cinemas around the world. Millions of dollars had already been spent on aborted promotional campaigns but the publicity drive was far from over. In fact, another huge promotional campaign would still be needed prior to the next (and hopefully last) release date. This cumulation of all of this was obviously now going to eat into any profits the movie would eventually accrue.

Some industry insiders were now very doubtful that No Time to Die would see any profit at all after all the money that had already been spent during the on/off promotional campaigns. The still uncertain nature of the cinema industry in these troubled times was another worrying factor. The pandemic stipulations and overall situation was not the same in all countries so an 'across the board' release for No Time to Die was by no means certain. Things were therefore still a trifle gloomy and up in the air when it came to No Time to Die and its theatrical release and potential in terms of cinema revenue. This is why there had been so much speculation about a home streaming release.

The main James Bond news was eventually the revelation that Amazon intended to purchase the ailing MGM in a deal worth billions. A major factor in Amazon's desire to go through with this transaction was the fact that ownership of MGM would obviously give them a sizeable stake in the James Bond franchise. Why else would Amazon be so enthusiastic to buy MGM? It's not as if Amazon were buying MGM to get the rights to make new Pink Panther movies! It was a slice of James Bond - one of the most famous and enduringly popular entertainment brands in history - which primarily motivated Amazon in this deal.

The commodity that all film companies and studios crave more than anything is a franchise. If you make a new movie with all original characters and an original script there is always the unavoidable element of the unknown. You don't know for sure how people will respond. More to the point, you don't know if they will respond at all. However, if you own something like James Bond or Star Wars then that element of risk is taken out of the equation. This is why studios love franchises and tend to flog them to death when they have one. Look at all these new Star Wars shows that are constantly appearing out of the woodwork now that Disney owns the rights. You can bet your life that there will be new Star Wars movies in the future too.

If you make a James Bond movie it may or may not make as much money as you projected or hope for but you can sleep easy safe in the knowledge that it assuredly won't bomb. A huge number of people will come out to watch a new James Bond film - no matter what the film is about or what the reviews are like. The same goes for Batman, Harry Potter, The Fast and the Furious, Spider-Man, and so on. There were soon a number of alarming articles fearing the worst from this proposed deal between MGM and Amazon. Scenarios were painted where Amazon launched endless Bond television shows, spin-offs, and maybe even Young Bond movies for their streaming service and generally ran the franchise into the ground.

The thought of the James Bond franchise being turned into Star Wars with TV shows, cartoons, and Moneypenny spin-off films was worrying to say the least. It was all though highly unlikely and more a case of slow day clickbait than probable reality. John Logan, who wrote on Skyfall and Spectre, was moved to pen a newspaper article in which he said the acquisition of MGM by Amazon gave him chills and that he had nightmares thinking about bungling Amazon executives clumsily meddling with the Bond franchise and trying to turn it into something it was never designed to be. What these stories and articles seemed to completely forget was that EON hadn't gone anywhere. Amazon would have to work as a studio partner to the formidable Barbara Broccoli and Barbara definitely wasn't the sort of person who would take a quiet back seat when it came to James Bond.

EON were pretty quick to dispense calming quotes in which they promised that, despite the prospect of Amazon (who obviously have a big streaming service) purchasing MGM, Bond would remain on the big screen and there would not be a tidal wave of James Bond themed spin-offs. EON assured fans they had ironclad guarantees they would retain artistic control of the franchise. EON's deal with MGM was always that they would split the profits but that EON made the really big creative decisions (like, for example, choosing which actor would play James Bond). EON clearly expected their arrangement with Amazon to run on similar lines. The chances of anyone not named Barbara Broccoli having the final say on the next Bond actor was unthinkable.

Not to say everyone was alarmed though by the news that Amazon now potentially had a stake in James Bond. In fact, some even saw this as a good thing because with Amazon's money behind them EON now had no excuses not to get these films out on a much more regular basis. And you could bet your life this is exactly what Amazon wanted. Amazon bean counters would clearly not be too thrilled or happy if EON maintained their recent pace of making a Bond film once in a blue moon. Bond fans who were long tired and bored of the 'gritty' melodramatic backstory Bond approach of EON in the Daniel Craig era could probably be forgiven too if they actually welcomed anything at all that might signify a slight change of direction.

A change of direction was coming though with or without Amazon. The next film (Bond 26 - though at this stage we were still waiting for Bond 25!) would have a brand new Bond actor.

It seemed highly unlikely and illogical that the next iteration of Bond would seek to overtly mimic the Craig era in any shape or form. The next era of Bond would have to forge its own path and do its own thing. No Time to Die was explicitly promoted as the final film for Daniel Craig and the concluding chapter in his saga. One (somewhat grating) teaser promo even pompously billed No Time to Die as the 'epic' conclusion as if it was the last part of a Star Wars or Lord of the Rings series.

There were a couple of risks in this strategy. The first risk was that most people probably couldn't even remember what happened in Spectre let alone the rest of the Craig era. The second risk was that No Time to Die might be overshadowed by the slowly escalating churn of articles concerning who might replace Daniel Craig as 007. There was the possibility that Bond 25 might lose some lustre and focus as eyes turned steadily towards Bond 26. In the end though none of these potential pitfalls proved to be major problems. Casual audiences didn't seem to care too much that the Craig films were not episodic and did not exist in isolation from one another in the way that the old Bond films mostly did. As for the background noise of Bond 26, the fanfare surrounding the long delayed Bond 25 proved more than sufficient to drown that out in the end.

It was reported that some edits were now required on No Time to Die to update the commercial product placement in the film. No Time to Die had sat in mothballs for so long that some of the technology gadgets involved in the movie were now at risk of being out of date. One tedious but unavoidable detail in modern Bond films is making sure that 007 has the absolute latest mobile telephone. No wonder some fans occasionally yearn for a period Bond film set in the Cold War where such tiresome matters were irrelevant.

It was reported in February that Mission: Impossible 7 (which was going to be split into two parts) was to take a production hiatus due to the pandemic. This was good news for MGM and EON because Mission: Impossible 7 was originally slated at one point to open only weeks after No Time to Die. This would now be (ahem) impossible. EON would obviously want as few big films as possible opening in the same period as No Time to Die - lest they should chip away at the potential box-office numbers.

Around this time, Christoph Waltz and Ralph Fiennes were both interviewed in the media. They confessed that - much to their frustration - they still hadn't been able to watch No Time to Die for themselves. They said they were as eager as the fans to see what the actual film was like. No Time to Die was like the gold in Fort Knox. It was firmly under lock and key. We knew that Daniel Craig had been able to watch a (not completely finished) print of No Time to Die but that evidently still wasn't the case for the rest of the cast.

Waltz echoed the views of Barbara Broccoli by saying that, in his opinion, James Bond films should stay on the big screen - where they belonged. Waltz definitely wasn't in favour of streaming No Time to Die. Waltz said that streaming No Time to Die at home would be as illogical as watching a TV show on the big screen. We understood his point but it didn't have perfect logic because a lot of television shows (like Stranger Things and Amazon's Lord of the Rings) were now lavish productions and better than most movies. They wouldn't be out of place at all on the big screen.

Many reports at this time indicated that No Time to Die would open at the end of September in a number of countries. That was certainly encouraging although Bond fans were probably reluctant to get their hopes up too high after all the previous false dawns. It was reported that Daniel Craig would be going on a worldwide media tour to promote the film and that MGM still had hopes it could top one billion dollars at the box-office. You could probably forgive Daniel Craig if he felt weary at the mere thought of this media tour but then this would be the last time. The next time a Bond film came out it would fall to his successor to do the endless rounds of chat shows, radio interviews, and press junkets. As for MGM's alleged hope that

No Time to Die might top one billion dollars, that seemed very unrealistic.

New stories in the media suggested that a £10 million premiere for No Time to Die was now being planned. EON were said to be very determined that, despite these troubled times, No Time to Die would not miss out on the traditional fanfare and extravagance of a Bond premiere. They wanted to give Daniel Craig one last special party and big night before he officially joined the ranks of ex-Bond actors. In the summer of 2021, there were also stories in the media that MGM were planning to campaign for No Time to Die to get an Oscar nomination for best picture. That seemed rather optimistic to say the least (with the best will in the world, a Bond film is never going to be in contention for a best film Oscar - no matter how good it might be) but did at least suggest that the studio had a lot of confidence in the quality of the film.

The cast interviews for No time to Die continued to trickle forth - despite the fact that there was still no sign of the actual film. Léa Seydoux talked about how Bond Girls had become Bond Women in the Craig era (it often seems that no modern Bond actress can do an interview without being discourteous all the Bond actresses that have come before them) and Michael G. Wilson chipped in to say that Madeleine Swann's relationship with Bond in the new film was complex and heart-rending. Wilson and Barbara Broccoli promised us that No Time to Die would be an epic love story sure to leave us in an emotional whirlpool.

The interviews all confirmed - not that any confirmation was really needed by this point - that No Time to Die was going to be a very direct sort of sequel to Spectre. We knew by now that Madeleine and Blofeld were both going to return. Michael G. Wilson promised that Blofeld would be bigger and badder than ever in the new film. We still had to wait though to see if this promise would be fulfilled. It's probably safe to say that EON were in one of their more pretentious moods in the long and winding preamble to No Time to Die. Broccoli and Wilson made it sound like they'd just produced The Godfather Part II.

You certainly couldn't accuse EON of not talking a good game. Still, this was all part of their job. They had to keep No Time to Die firmly in the public eye and as good a way as any to do that was to conduct a lot of interviews and constantly say how brilliant the film was. Broccoli and Wilson seemed to be rather enjoying this last bittersweet go around with Daniel Craig. It was evident that they would miss their leading man. Daniel Craig was much more than an employee to Broccoli and Wilson. He was a friend and even a co-producer on the films. The challenge EON would soon face would be to find the right replacement for Daniel Craig. Who that next actor might be was still in the unknown realm of complete guesswork at this point.

Cary Fukunaga was now interviewed by Total Film as part of the endless promotional campaign for No Time to Die and revealed that before Danny Boyle was hired he had gone out to dinner with Barbara Broccoli to discuss potentially directing the next film. Fukunaga, intriguingly, said that at the time they assumed that Daniel Craig wasn't coming back so actually discussed who might replace him. Bond fans would doubtless have loved to be a fly on the wall for that conversation! Fukunaga was diplomatic enough not to divulge to Total Film any of the names they discussed as potential successors to Daniel Craig. Despite initially being overlooked, Fukunaga evidently made a good impression on Barbara Broccoli over dinner because he was drafted in fairly swiftly when Danny Boyle departed Bond 25.

Articles purporting to having any insight into who the next 007 might be at this point continued to be inconsequential and meaningless. Tom Hardy, as ever, was endlessly touted - despite the fact that he was 44 years-old and liable to be three or four years older than that by the time Bond 26 saw the light of day. Tom Hardy was simply not a viable contender anymore. Age also disqualified Michael Fassbender - another fixture in these next Bond ruminations. No one disputes that

Fassbender is a fine actor who probably would have been a very good James Bond (look how suave and polished Fassbender is as Lieutenant Archie Hicox in the Quentin Tarantino film Inglourious Basterds) but Fassbender was a year older than Tom Hardy and so could now be filed as another potential Bond who aged out of contention during the Daniel Craig era. Fassbender had already ruled himself out of contention anyway in a 2016 Esquire interview. He appeared to be bemused that anyone even thought he was in the running.

James Norton (an unremarkable English actor who must have an exceptionally talented agent to constantly feature so prominently in next James Bond articles) was mystifyingly ubiquitous once again in such puff pieces. Many articles had him as the favourite and Norton, if his comments are anything to go by, certainly seemed up for playing 007. A relatively new name in these escalating clickbait temptations was Regé-Jean Page. Page is best known for his role in the period drama Bridgerton and now found himself heavily touted to be the first black James Bond actor. Page was the perfect age (not too old but not TOO young either) but did he have the necessary acting chops and screen presence for Bond? Questions like this would be for EON and their casting director to endlessly ponder and debate over in the months and (knowing EON) years to come as they waded through the sizeable male acting pool in Britain and beyond.

One name who seemed to fallen completely by the wayside in the great game of next Bond casting bingo was Tom Hiddleston. Hiddleston seemed to be rarely mentioned anymore. It suddenly seemed a long time ago now when that flurry of speculation post-Spectre gave the impression that Hiddleston was at EON's HQ having his tux fitted. Many of the names dubiously linked to the part in the media continued to be unrealistic red herrings. The respected and always busy Irish actor Cillian Murphy, thanks to Peaky Blinders, was frequently touted for Bond in the media but Murphy was even older than Tom Hardy so very unlikely to be feasible. Though a fine actor, the diminutive Murphy was even shorter than Daniel Craig at 5'7. He definitely wouldn't have passed Cubby Broccoli's famous height criteria.

One man who wasn't shy in touting himself for Bond was the Outlander star Sam Heughan. In fact, Heughan rarely seemed to shut up about his aspiration to be the next 007. Heughan was certainly familiar to EON because he'd been one of the actors they'd looked before Daniel Craig was cast in Casino Royale. The problem for Heughan was that EON never seem too keen on actors who suggest themselves for the part (see Gerard Butler or Tom Hiddleston) and it is therefore best for potential Bond candidates to play coy and hard to get. Just avoid the subject altogether and keep your mouth shut is the most logical advice. The other problem facing Sam Heughan was that he was in his early forties now and liable to be far too old to be starting out as Bond by the time that Bond 26 finally began to rumble towards any sort of start date. It was highly doubtful that EON were going to plunge straight into Bond 26 once No Time to Die's release, promotion, and cinema run was finally done and dusted.

The one name above all who continued to dominate the next Bond article fluff so beloved of tabloids and clickbait entertainment sites was Idris Elba. Iris Elba was British and a versatile and charismatic actor with a commanding screen presence. He could be tough, convincingly do action, and handle humour. He was also a proven leading man. On the face of it, Elba seemed to possess most of the qualities one would look for in a James Bond actor. He ticked most of those 007 boxes. There was one big problem though - and it was a problem that these clickbait articles curiously seemed to completely gloss over or ignore altogether. The problem was that Elba was only about four years younger than Daniel Craig. What would be the point in replacing Craig with an actor who was nearly as old as him? That would appear to be almost completely pointless.

The Craig era had mined heavily into the theme of Bond being old, tired, retired, and clapped-out so it seemed very logical that the best way for the next iteration to distinguish itself from the previous era (and therefore immediately establish its own sense of identity) would be to cast a much younger actor than usual and go for someone in their mid to early thirties - or even younger. While there is obviously an enjoyable cinema tradition of older male action stars (John Wayne, Liam Neeson, Charles Bronson, Harrison Ford, Sly Stallone etc) it didn't seem like a wagon that the Bond franchise should seek to permanently attach itself to.

If Idris Elba were to be signed up as the next Bond at this juncture he would be about the same age Roger Moore was in Octopussy or A View to a Kill by the time his second film came out. That would be a very short-sighted and strange sort of casting strategy and as such remained - despite the endless speculation - very unlikely. In her many quotes concerning the next Bond actor, Barbara Broccoli was always at pains to explain that when you cast Bond you are casting someone for four or five films. You need to find someone who can play James Bond for a decade or more. It was very doubtful then that Barbara was sitting in an EON office watching showreels of Tom Hardy or Idris Elba. Her gaze was much more likely to be the rising generation of British actors still in their thirties.

The main concern at this time for MGM and EON was still the possibility of story leaks. Call sheets had revealed that Madeline would have a child in the film and so there was naturally much speculation that this would turn out to be Bond's child. There had also been details that Billy Magnusson's CIA agent Ash would be a villain. Most of the really big secrets (chiefly the ending) of No Time to Die were still under wraps though - which was no mean feat given how long ago this film was actually completed.

The real doomsday scenario was that a copy of the film would somehow leak online before its release. This is not completely unheard of in the modern film industry. Films like Super 8 and Zombieland were leaked online before they hit cinemas. A print of The Expendables 3 turned up online a few weeks before its release and was downloaded millions of times (which was obviously a complete disaster for that film's box-office). The security surrounding No Time to Die was stringent enough though to prevent this digital nightmare scenario from happening.

Most of the speculation concerning No Time to Die naturally surrounded its ending. There was a lot of anticipation concerning the way the Craig era would end. Would it be a happy ending? Would it be a downbeat Logan style ending? There were even somewhat fanciful rumours that No Time to Die would end by seguing into the start of Dr No - thus bringing the Bond series full circle. All bets were off at this stage. No one quite knew how No Time to Die was going to end. There were stories too that Cary Fukunaga had shot (rather like 'who shot J.R' in the TV soap opera Dallas!) several different endings to the movie in order to obfuscate the real ending he planned to use. Daniel Craig said that No Time to Die went through four different scripts before the cameras started rolling so many different endings were considered or proposed before the final decision was made.

Purvis and Wade, the regular (and often much maligned) writers on Bond for many years now, were interviewed at this time. They said they spent months in an EON 'attic' with Cary Fukunaga trying to knock the script by John Hodge (which was obviously written for the aborted Danny Boyle film) into shape. What they basically ended up with was a completely new story. Boyle's Russian themed script was kicked into the long grass. Fukunaga said that coming up with the ending for No Time to Die had caused the biggest headaches in the writer's room. Barbara Broccoli and Daniel Craig both had some input into this ending - which suggested it was rather bold and atypical as far as Bond films go. Nothing went into a Bond film these days unless it was approved by Daniel Craig. It seemed impossible to think that another James Bond actor would ever wield such power in the franchise again.

Purvis and Wade promised that No Time to Die would feel completely different from the previous films - despite the fact that it would be heavily connected to the last movie (Spectre) in particular. This was a theme that Michael G. Wilson articulated in a press interview around this time. Wilson said the delicate balancing act with a Bond movie is to give people what they want but also a few things that feel different. You have to, according to Wilson, straddle both the needs of Bond loyalists and the sensibility of the times. It was certainly a gamble making such an overt sequel to Spectre because that film, certainly in comparison to Skyfall, was quite poorly received. Spectre would also be ancient history by the time that No Time to Die finally arrived. Who can remember the precise details of Spectre anymore? Bond fans maybe (at a stretch) but certainly not casual audiences.

Not to say that Spectre doesn't have its fans. That film, while hardly classic Bond, was at least slightly less angsty than other Craig entries and somewhat more of a straight forward adventure. Spectre did struggle though with the Craig era obsession of connecting all of these films together into one big story. Whether or not EON were ultimately successful in this artistic strategy this is open to question. It was apparent on Spectre that Sam Mendes was always groping somewhat to find a reason for the film's existence or his own participation. When he made Skyfall, Mendes had a solid concept and clarity of purpose. He never quite seemed to find any of that raison d'etre on Spectre and admitted as much in later interviews.

The connected story arc on the Craig film was clearly influenced by modern trends - most famously seen in the Marvel universe. The Marvel films are all connected. If you are making, for example, a Star Wars trilogy then your story has to be connected (the recent Star Wars trilogy plainly failed to connect all the dots in a satisfying way in the end after a promising start) with a beginning, middle, and end. James Bond has never required this approach though and got by perfectly well with largely disconnected stand alone adventures. In a sense then the Daniel Craig era was something of an experiment. It felt very self-contained when contrasted against the franchise as a whole.

In a Total Film piece, Michael G. Wilson described the Daniel Craig era of Bond as a 'miniseries within the series'. That was as good a way as any of putting it. The Craig era was obstinately its own thing in the end. Craig's era would be the first time an incarnation of James Bond got both a beginning and a full stop. With the other Bond actors we just join their 007 somewhere in the middle of their career and their age is never mentioned. Roger Moore does not play Bond any differently in a View to a Kill - despite the fact he is knocking on a bit and clearly at the end of his tenure. A View to a Kill makes no reference at all to Bond being old or near retirement.

Never before No Time to Die had a Bond movie been so explicitly promoted as the last hurrah for an actor. Daniel Craig was rather unique in the franchise in the way that he was able to do things on his own terms - even to the point of having a special farewell movie. The only other time in the history of the franchise when it was fairly (though not conclusively) apparent that an actor was making his last film was Roger Moore in A View to a Kill. Given that Roger was 57 years-old at the time it was probably inevitable that he wouldn't be back. The film was not marketed as Roger Moore's last film though. It was simply marketed as another Bond movie.

In an interview, Daniel Craig described the themes of No Time to Die as 'love and family' (which felt like pretty odd sort of themes for a Bond movie!) and said he decided to come back and do one more because he was promised the film would have some emotional heft and drama and complete the story his character had begun in Casino Royale. Craig was persuaded by Barbara Broccoli that there was still some story left to tell. He liked the idea of putting a big full stop on his era. Craig was clearly not entirely satisfied with Spectre and had therefore been tempted by the offer to have one more final go around which would definitely end his era. He had unfinished business and No Time to Die would rectify that and give him closure.

Though the production of the films in Daniel Craig's era was increasingly sporadic and never really threatened to beat Roger Moore's seven film record, Craig's longevity in the role was still fairly remarkable. He became Bond in 2005 and here we were in 2021 with him still officially the 007 of record. One could argue that the intermittent and sporadic nature of Bond films in the Craig era as a whole (prior to No Time to Die, EON had only delivered two Bond films in about ten years) had made them feel more like big events because they arrived so infrequently! It would certainly be interesting to see if Bond films on a more regular basis (every two years - as was custom in the old days) again in the future would affect their box-office or sense of importance in any way.

Specifically because of the infrequent nature of Bond films these days, not everyone was gloomy about the box-office challenges facing No Time to Die in these precarious times. In fact, some analysts argued that the many frustrating delays the film had endured might actually work to its advantage. The theory suggested that the long wait might serve to make No Time to Die a bigger event. The on/off nature of the promotional campaigns had kept the film in the public eye for many months now. No Time to Die was sort of like an anticipated dinner that had been simmering in a pot for hours. So, to continue my somewhat clumsy food/Bond metaphor, maybe by the time the dish was eventually served perhaps everyone would be much hungrier than usual and more grateful for the dinner?

The question of why the Bond films had become so sporadic in the Daniel Craig era was certainly interesting. It plainly wasn't a case of laziness and inertia because Barbara Broccoli was still energetic and ambitious. She had produced other movies outside of the 007 franchise and also worked in the theatre. It wasn't as if Barbara made a Bond film and then sat in her house in her pyjamas watching television for five years before reluctantly dragging herself off the sofa to begin work on the next one. The sporadic nature of the modern Bond movies was a confluence of four factors. The first was some mild background studio turmoil - though this was a picnic compared to the litigation which kept Bond off the big screen in the early 1990s. Things were not entirely stable behind the scenes but EON had endured worse in the past.

The second factor was Daniel Craig's increasing reluctance to commit himself to another film. This was most evident after Spectre. Exhausted and nursing a number of injuries, Daniel Craig was more than happy to walk away from 007 in 2015 and spend more time with his family. The third factor was connected to the second factor. The third factor was Barbara Broccoli's refusal to countenance anyone other than Daniel Craig playing James Bond. This meant that Barbara was perfectly willing to keep the franchise in stasis for years while she waited for Craig to make a decision on whether to come back. This is definitely not something you could imagine Cubby Broccoli and Harry Saltzman putting up with. If they had a reluctant 007 actor who wanted increasingly long breaks between movies and complained about being tired then they would have strapped him in the ejector seat and cast someone more enthusiastic for the role.

The fourth factor in the frustratingly irregular arrival of modern Bond films was a sense that Barbara Broccoli had a tendency to overthink everything. She always seemed to act as if a Bond film took years of torturous preparation, writing, and creative soul-searching before it could go before a camera. In reality, it needn't be that complicated. Look at the way they churn out the Marvel movies on a regular basis - and most of those have been pretty good too. While no one would want a film to be rushed, most Bond fans would probably suggest that EON should be (now that the pandemic seems to hopefully behind us) getting these movies out on a much more regular basis. Besides, it isn't as if the longer gestation periods have even guaranteed precise or perfect preparation. Spectre and No Time to Die were both subject to last minute script revisions.

Total Film were impressed by the sets they witnessed during the Pinewood studio visit they were allowed. The production and set designers on No Time to Die had clearly done an amazing job creating some beautiful sets. The Cuban set was quite incredible and there was a happy retro whiff of Ken Adam to some of the other interiors they caught a glimpse of. By this stage though Bond fans were getting a bit tired reading about Cuban themed sets, Daniel Craig's injuries, Madeleine Swann, Billie Eilish, and how tough and complex Bond Girls, sorry, Bond Woman, were these days. They simply wanted to watch the film before they died of old age. Thankfully, the end was almost in sight now. The waiting game didn't have too much longer to play out.

Regarding the media rumours that Rami Malek's mysterious villain Safin was really Dr No, both EON and Malek were remaining coy for now on that front. EON seemed to be enjoying the speculation and theories concerning No Time to Die. They were still the only people who knew if any of these theories were actually true. In July, Ana de Armas did a magazine interview and we were subjected to yet more waffle about how she would play a different type of Bond girl for the 21st Century (whatever that is supposed to mean). Ana de Armas said that Paloma was quite unlike any other Bond Woman we'd seen before because she was (wait for it) tough and complex. Ana de Armas could evidently be chalked up as yet another modern Bond actress who had apparently never heard of Diana Rigg or Honor Blackman.

New posters at this time stated that No Time to Die would be released in October. At this stage, No Time to Die was like the Bond film that cried wolf when it came to release dates but things were certainly looking far less bleak than they had done before. The James Bond Twitter then put out a No Time to Die 'sizzle reel' confirming that it was all systems go for an October release. There were stories too around this time about how No Time to Die would have to make one billion dollars to show any profit because of its enormous production costs and lengthy stop start promotional campaigns. Given the uncertain nature of the box-office (and the cinema industry as a whole) this would be a stern (and most likely impossible) challenge to say the least. One advantage Bond did enjoy though was that it tended to skew towards an older demographic. It wasn't quite so reliant on young audiences in the way that other movies sometimes were.

There was more sign of light at the end of a very long tunnel when news emerged that No Time to Die would have its world premiere at the Royal Albert Hall in London on the 28th of September. The Royal Albert Hall is a concert hall on the northern edge of South Kensington. It was opened by Queen Victoria in 1871 and has been for many years the venue for the BBC Proms. This grand and beautiful building has been host to pop concerts and even boxing matches over the years. The likes of Lennox Lewis, Prince Naseem Hamed, and Frank Bruno all had fights there. Muhammad Ali once famously boxed an exhibition at the Royal Albert Hall. The after party for No Time to Die would take place at the Natural History Museum. EON were certainly pushing the boat out for this premiere.

Cinemas in Britain and Japan soon began selling tickets for No Time to Die screenings. It wasn't Bond fans who were the most impatient to see No Time to Die released by this point but cinema owners. Cinema owners in Britain (where modern Bond films traditionally did very big business - around $100 million) in particular were desperately relying on No Time to Die to save their businesses and perhaps even the industry as a whole. James Bond was being counted on to provide the shot in the arm that this flagging industry was in dire need of. Cinema owners had absolutely everything crossed that No Time to Die would be able to enjoy a long and uninterrupted theatrical run.

During the pandemic many wondered if cinemas, in an age of home streaming and televisions the size of sheds, would increasingly become a thing of the past - even when things did go back to normal. We've all had bad experiences at the cinema. Some idiot behind you constantly talking or eating through the film. Someone in the next seat endlessly checking their phone. Bored kids. People constantly getting up to use the toilet. Going to the cinema can be annoying. Watching a film in comfort at home has some obvious advantages. However, nothing will ever beat the big screen experience. If you've only ever watched films like 2001: A Space Odyssey or Gravity on the small screen then I'm afraid to say that you haven't truly watched those films. The big screen was where James Bond belonged and where he would stay so long as Barbara Broccoli had anything to do with it.

A new official synopsis for the film was now released by EON. There wasn't much that was new in this synopsis but, encouragingly, it was evidence that this latest release date seemed on much firmer ground than the previous aborted ones had been. 'James Bond (Daniel Craig) has left active service and is enjoying a tranquil life in Jamaica. His peace is short-lived when his old friend Felix Leiter (Jeffrey Wright) from the CIA turns up asking for help, and M (Ralph Fiennes) also looks to bring 007 back for a new mission. When Bond encounters a new 00 named Nomi (Lashana Lynch), who has replaced him as the top agent, he learns she isn't impressed by his past achievements. The mission, which is to rescue a kidnapped scientist, turns out to be far more treacherous than expected, leading Bond onto the trail of a mysterious villain named Safin (Rami Malek), who is armed with dangerous new technology.'

By now, a raft of new trailers were emerging in different territories and it was announced that the film had been rated PG-13 in the United States. No Time to Die was finally - FINALLY! - nearing an actual release. One factor worrying the studio bean counters at this point though was that No Time to Die still had no scheduled release date in China. China is an increasingly important film market these days - as one might expect of such a populous and increasingly wealthy country which is destined to become the largest economy in the world. In some circumstances a film can even bomb in North America but then recoup its production costs in China. That was something which was completely unheard of not so long ago. Spectre had made nearly $90 million in China and No Time to Die was desperately hoping for a decent wedge of that Chinese money too because it would need every penny it could muster.

At this time the No Time to Die merch was ramping up too. The 007 Store had begun selling Safin No Time to Die Noh masks. They were priced at £295. Nearly £300 for a Safin mask? I think I'll pass on that one thank you very much. No Time to Die merch would include Cashmere clothing, an Aston Martin diecast model, Funko Pop figures, Tote bags, coins, an Aston Martin toy model with Playmobil figures of James Bond, Goldfinger, and Oddjob (what Bond fan worth their salt wouldn't be tempted by that one!), and much more besides.

All the enthusiasm now generated by the imminent release of No Time to Die did not fly by without one party pooper though. The Hollywood Reporter ran a gloomy article in which they said that No Time to Die's projected release date was risky because a resurgence of the pandemic could wreak havoc if it arrived at the worst possible time. That worst possible time would obviously be shortly after No Time To Die had finally opened - a disaster of a scenario indeed. The Hollywood Reporter suggested that MGM and EON now had no choice though but to stick to the 'risky' September/October release date because things might be even worse early next year in terms of the pandemic.

Another salient factor in why MGM and EON couldn't delay No Time to Die forever (No Time to Die Forever sounds like a title for a Bond film!) was the fact each time a release date was aborted this cost the studio many extra millions because they then had to launch ANOTHER fresh promotional campaign when the next release date swung around again. The delays were in danger, if alarmist reports were true, of crippling the finances of MGM. This would not be a problem if they were owned by Amazon. There was also the very real risk of people getting bored of No Time to Die - despite the fact that they hadn't even seen the film! After several aborted promotional campaigns people could be forgiven if it sometimes felt as if they HAD seen the film and that it was already yesterday's news.

One disadvantage faced by No Time to Die is that, unlike big Disney movies, it didn't have the option of a simultaneous streaming release to maximise profits. Barbara Broccoli would never have agreed to such a strategy. Broccoli and Wilson were interviewed yet again at this time (in fairness it might have been an old interview held back for months) and made clear that, despite the Amazon deal, they had no interest in Bond television shows and spin-off films. Wilson said they had always been against such projects. Michael's memory was clearly playing tricks on him because he was involved in the 1990s James Bond Jr cartoon and he and Barbara tried to make an aborted Jinx spin-off film with Halle Berry. *

There were inklings of potential trouble for No Time to Die when it was announced that Australia and New Zealand had pushed their release dates of the movie back to November because of the pandemic. This was a pain for Bond fans in those countries because their chances of avoiding spoilers were now greatly impacted. MGM had everything crossed that this wasn't a portent of things to come. Late in August it was announced that MGM planned to release Addams Family 2 in both cinemas and on pay-per-view at the same time. This was seen as reasonable evidence for the theory that MGM would have been happy to employ the same strategy for No Time to Die but that this strategy had been vetoed by EON.

* The aborted Jinx spin-off film had a script by Neal Purvis and Robert Wade and Stephen Frears was signed to direct. It apparently had a $90 million budget. Halle Berry was apparently enthusiastic for the project and Michael Madsen was being lined up to reprise his role from Die Another Day in support. Neal Purvis and Robert Wade said the story was a Bourne style thriller set in Europe.

MGM pulled the plug on the Jinx project in the end. They are alleged to have got very cold feet after the poor box-office returns of female led action movies like the Lara Croft and Charlie's Angels sequels. It could be the case that the backlash against Die Another Day (a film which earned decent reviews upon release but became increasingly disliked and picked apart thereafter) was also a factor in the Jinx movie being cancelled. The scrapped Jinx movie is definitely a strange footnote in the history of Bond. It never sounded like a very good idea in the first place so it isn't surprising at all that it got canned in the end. The film getting as far as it did was probably a result of Barbara Broccoli liking both the idea of doing a female fronted action film and working with Halle Berry again. Berry was a pretty big star at the time.

The decision to axe Jinx had unfortunate consequences for Halle Berry because she signed up to make a 2004 Catwoman movie instead. Catwoman was directed by Pitof (a French director who goes by a single name and probably hasn't worked since this disaster was unleashed on an unsuspecting public) and written by John Rogers, John Brancato and Michael Ferris. This megabomb cleaned up at the Razzies and was a critical and box-office disaster. Ever since Batman Returns the character of Catwoman was slated for a spin-off film but by the time it arrived any connection to the Batman universe was gone. This Catwoman is not Selina Kylie but someone called Patience Phillips. Halle Berry (who had just won an Oscar at the time) was the unfortunate actress roped into this legendary misfire to take the lead. The sad thing about Catwoman is that it had a big budget and quite a lot of hype. The actual film was a big disappointment to say the least.

Berry's Patience Philips character works for a cosmetic company but discovers that a new age defying beauty cream might have some alarming side effects. Profits are profits and Patience is bumped off by the greedy company for her troubles but - after apparently drowning - is resurrected by an Egyptian Mau cat and develops cat type powers. She's soon out for revenge and dispensing terrible cat themed puns. You can tell that Catwoman isn't working at all because even Halle Berry isn't having much fun and delivers a forced performance that suggests the actress is wondering how on earth she got herself into this mess. The film has no story and is awash with subpar CGI of the era (the sort that sometimes blighted the Matrix sequel - only worse). Nothing seems real in the film and the hokey artificial backdrops and CG action both grate in the end and add to the cartoonish aura of the film.

The script gives Catwoman some terrible jokes and bland villains (hello to Sharon Stone) and the action is never terribly exciting or very well choreographed. The film doesn't work on any particular level and the jokey tongue-in-cheek approach it strives for falls flat. Catwoman's outfit consists of not much more than a leather bra and tight trousers. The sight of Halle Berry in fetish clothing is probably the only reason anyone would have to want to watch this film. It's a strange and curious treatment of the Catwoman property and isn't even interesting enough to have gathered any 'so bad it's good' cult appeal over the years. Catwoman has the air of a project that was rushed into production without any clear sense of direction or noticeable knowledge of the Catwoman character. No wonder it bombed. The only thing anyone really remembers about Catwoman now is that Halle Berry (gamely) turned up at the Razzies to collect her award.

# CHAPTER TWO - THE RELEASE

The latest (and hopefully LAST) promotional campaign for No Time to Die was at full throttle by now. Footage from the film was shown at CinemaCon and the 007 themed social media feeds were more furiously active than ever. Lashana Lynch was interviewed by the Los Angeles Times and we were reminded (lest we should have forgotten) for the millionth time that she plays a 00 agent named Nomi in the film. Lynch was certainly getting more than her fair share of ink in the media. The promotional campaign virtually gave one the impression that

Nomi was very prominent in the film and would be on the screen all the time. Would this hype be justified though?

The final international trailers were released and a documentary about Daniel Craig's Bond titled Being James Bond was released on Apple near the start of September. After an early section on the infamous CraigNotBond affair and the initial media criticism of the casting, Being James Bond was a disappointingly brief (45 minutes) and bland victory lap through the Daniel Craig era which didn't really tell you anything you didn't already know if you followed the production of those films (and most Bond fans obviously WOULD have followed those productions). The documentary basically consists of clips and production footage from the last four Bond films while Barbara Broccoli and Michael G. Wilson endlessly talk about how brilliant, remarkable, talented, incredible, and amazing Daniel Craig is.

Of most interest in the documentary is the footage from Craig's 007 screen test for Casino Royale. EON tend not to release much screen test footage (you can find those of James Brolin, Sam Neil, and Roger Green online but the rest are locked in a vault) so this was certainly novel and fascinating. The Bond screentests are elaborate affairs on the evidence we see here with a sizeable crew. Martin Campbell could be seen giving Craig direction on the set. Daniel Craig had quite long hair during his test because he was shooting a movie called The Invasion at the time and so wasn't allowed to get his hair cut.

The documentary didn't really mention the Bond franchise as a whole much or put Craig's era in a wider context but then this was supposed to be a special celebration of Craig's tenure so you couldn't really begrudge them that single focus. In the documentary, Barbara Broccoli said that Daniel Craig was the only actor she wanted for Casino Royale and that they actually had to be persuaded and badgered by the studio to test some of the other actors. It seems then that none of the other Casino Royale contenders (like Henry Cavill and Sam Worthington) actually stood a cat in hell's chance of playing Bond in the film.

Daniel Craig said that he studied all the early online criticism of his casting and that it only served to make him work harder and try and prove everyone wrong. Being James Bond is hagiographic to say the least (Barbara even tries to pretend that Quantum of Solace was really good) but it was just designed as a nice little tribute to the departing Daniel Craig and a bonus for Bond fans as they counted down the last days to No Time to Die's release. As such, it would be churlish to be too critical of its shortcomings.

The promotional campaign continued to ramp up at this time with numerous featurettes and commercials. Aston Martin and Omega also both released product commercials to promote the film. There are few marketing campaigns in the world of film which can match Bond when it comes to a media blitz and so it was with No Time to Die. By this time you'd have had to be a hermit living in a cave with no electricity not to know that a new James Bond film was about to be released. No Time to Die was everywhere. This campaign was above and beyond anything we'd seen before for No Time to Die. It was the final mighty (and expensive) push before the film was sent out to cinemas around the globe.

It had been six long years since Spectre came out. One of the byproducts of No Time To Die taking taking so long to come out was that it threatened to alter the casting landscape entirely when it came to the next Bond actor. If, as was planned or assumed at one point, Daniel Craig had called it quits after Spectre then potential 007 candidates like Aidan Turner, Henry Cavill, and Dan Stevens would have been the perfect age circa 2015/2016 to replace him. Now though, with production on the next Bond (the one after No Time to Die) not likely to commence until at least 2024, those actors (should they be interested - we know from his comments that Henry Cavill, for one, would be up for Bond) now faced the very real prospect of being aged out of contention. We now didn't have the faintest idea who Craig's replacement might potentially be. The chances of a youngish relative unknown seemed to be increasing all the time.

MGM and EON must have breathed a heavy sigh of relief when China lifted its temporary embargo on Western films and cleared No Time to Die for release. Chinese cinemas had been giving the priority to Chinese films to support their own film industry in these troubled economic times. The policy was sort of like import controls - only with movies instead of goods. The Chinese revenue that No Time to Die was liable to generate would, as we have noted, be desperately needed. By now, cinemas in the United States had begun selling tickets for screenings of No Time to Die. It was unthinkable that the plug would be pulled again at this late stage. MGM and EON had gambled all of their poker chips on the September/October release.

Cary Fukunaga was interviewed by The Hollywood Reporter as No Time to Die finally geared up for its imminent and long delayed release. By now, Fukunaga had moved onto other things. He was working on Masters of the Air - a Tom Hanks and Steven Spielberg produced miniseries sequel to Band of Brothers and The Pacific. Fukunaga was directing the first three episodes of Masters of the Air. The Hollywood Reporter article suggested that Danny Boyle's proposed Bond film had been more 'whimsical' than the one we were about to get and this was a salient factor in Boyle's departure. Fukunaga's sensibility was to make a dark and brooding sort of Bond film and this tied in much more with what Barbara Broccoli and Daniel Craig wanted.

During one of his many published interviews at this time, Fukunaga seemed to have an unnecessary dig at the late Sir Roger Moore when he said didn't like the 'eyebrow up' version of Bond. Fukunaga denied that Rami Malek was playing Dr No in No Time to Die but some wondered if this was misdirection. We'd know for sure soon enough. During the interview with The Hollywood Reporter, the 'Weinstein era' was mentioned (the powerful Hollywood producer Harvey Weinstein abused his power with sexual assaults on dozens of famous women in the film industry - the shocking thing about the Weinstein case is that he got away with it for so long) and in response Cary Fukunaga said that some changes to the Bond franchise were necessary in an age of #MeToo.

Fukunaga then said that Sean Connery's Bond was a rapist - although, unhelpfully, he didn't seem to remember which film he was actually talking about when it came to the evidence for this. As we shall see, Fukunaga's interview with The Hollywood Reporter - where he depicted himself as a great towering beacon of light in the ongoing struggle against sexism and misogyny - would become darkly ironic after the dust settled on No Time to Die because several women later came forward with accusations and allegations of sexual misconduct and bullying against him. Nick Cuse, who did some writing on No Time to Die, later called Cary Fukunaga the "worst human being I have ever met in my life."

Barbara Broccoli happily joined Cary Fukunaga in the pile-on against the old Bond films and basically suggested they were all sexist. It would seem to be stating the bleeding obvious to point out that films made nearly sixty years might seem a bit dated in places today in the realm of sex and gender politics. As such, Broccoli's offhand digs at the old Bond films felt completely unnecessary and rather disrespectful. It always struck one as slightly odd that Barbara never quite seemed to realise that whenever she had a snooty dig at at an old Bond film she was, by association, also being somewhat critical of her father. Cubby was obviously the producer on all of those eye-rolling sexist silly old movies which so offended and amused her now.

There was a curious phenomenon in the Daniel Craig era where the modern EON sometimes appeared almost embarrassed by the fact that Bond films existed long before Daniel Craig. It was as if Barbara Broccoli dearly wished that Daniel Craig had been the ONLY person who'd ever played Bond. One other curious facet of the Craig era was that neither

EON nor critics ever seemed to give Timothy Dalton much credit for portraying a more grounded and 'gritty' version of Bond decades before Daniel Craig came along. * To hear Barbara talk about the Bond series you'd sometimes think they were all mostly like Carry On films before 2006.

By now a positive blizzard of international TV spots and trailers was in full flow. This definitely felt like the point of no return now. Lashana Lynch was featured in a Daily Mail profile and Barbara Broccoli suggested in the article that Nomi could feature in the next film too. This felt like Barbara being diplomatic rather than anything that might actually happen in reality. Given that the next film was likely to be a clean slate with a new Bond it seemed highly unlikely that they were going to saddle the next reboot (and a reboot was surely on cards again post-Craig) with any characters from No Time to Die.

Barbara repeated her stance that the next Bond would not be a woman and that it would be much better to write good new female characters rather than turn old male characters female. These comments by Barbara Broccoli were seemingly ignored by oddsmakers and punters though because names like Lydia West, Gillian Anderson, Suranne Jones, and (inevitably) Lashana Lynch continued to feature on next Bond betting pages. Doctor Who, Higgins in Magnum, Pinhead in Hellraiser, Starbuck in Battlestar Galactica. All of these characters and more had gone from male to female in reboots. James Bond would not be joining them though.

Cinemas in Britain had now began hiring extra staff to cope with all the forthcoming screenings of No Time to Die. Advance ticket sales were excellent and cinemas were looking forward to a big opening weekend. Cary Fukunaga was featured in the Radio Times and said he was given a generous amount of freedom to craft No Time to Die's story in the way that he wanted. Fukunaga said that one of the main 'anchor points' (which wasn't up for debate) was that he had to give Craig's Bond a definitive sort of ending in this film. Comments like this led to speculation that Bond might actually die in the new movie. The producers surely wouldn't be this bold. Would they?

It was now Christmas Eve as far as No Time to Die was concerned. It still had all the mystique and wonder of an unwrapped present sitting under the Christmas tree. The Guardian found the time to publish an article suggesting the Bond franchise was an anachronism and should come to an end. This was hardly original. Articles like this concerning the Bond franchise had been around for decades. The Guardian had probably been writing this same article since Roger Moore was Bond. You could file this Guardian article in the drawer marked tedious clickbait. Cary Fukunaga continued to be a busy and in demand man and was interviewed for Yahoo. He said that the only thing that changed during the long delays and lockdowns was that a visual effects shot was given a bit of a polish. Besides that, nothing had been changed at all. The vague stories alleging that reshoots had occurred were patently false.

Fukunaga said that he thought the next Bond actor should be completely different to Daniel Craig because you didn't want to serve up exactly the same thing to fans all the time. The franchise would have to make the next era markedly different to freshen things up. This was still the far flung future though as far as Bond went. Michael G. Wilson and Barbara Broccoli said they still hadn't given any serious thought yet to who the next James Bond actor might be. They simply wanted to enjoy this one last hurrah for Daniel Craig and worry about the future when the time came. Idris Elba continued to be the ubiquitous focal point of next Bond articles. A media story at this time also suggested that Elba had been offered the part of the Bond villain in the next movie. Given that the next Bond film had yet to be written this story was clearly unverified.

A few days before the films opened, Barbara Broccoli and Michael G. Wilson appeared on Radio 4. As you might imagine, they were full of praise for their departing star as his final bow finally prepared for release. Wilson said that Craig would leave big shoes to fill and it was hard to imagine how they be able to replace him. Broccoli said they were lucky to get Craig because he was very reluctant to take the role at first. She explained that his initial reluctance was because he was a private person and feared that it would turn his life upside down. I suspect that Daniel Craig's accountant and bank manager were eternally relieved that he overcame these reservations and signed on the dotted line in the end! Craig now had a reported net worth of $160 million. A considerable amount of that money was obviously a direct result of playing James Bond in five films.

In today's money, Sean Connery earned about $3.5 million per Bond film. When you take out George Lazenby, Sean Connery is actually the lowest paid of the Bond actors. This is why Connery seemed to end up disliking Cubby Broccoli and Harry Saltzman. Connery felt that he never got a fair share of the incredible profits that the Bond movies made in the 1960s. Adjusted for inflation, the most financially successful James Bond film of all time is 1965's Thunderball. Connery was James Bond during the peak Bondmania years so you can understand why he felt he should have been paid more. Roger Moore was paid double Sean's salary on his Bond films. By way of contrast, Daniel Craig was paid an average of around $10 million per Bond film and also got a cut of the profits. In his career after James Bond, it is claimed that Sean Connery was very forensic when it came to profit share deals on movies and even hired accountants for the specific task of investigating the profits of each film he made to make sure he wasn't being short-changed.

There was an interesting sort of parallel to Craig several months later when the Irish actor Aidan Turner, who has long been a fan favourite to be the next Bond thanks to his Dalton-esque good looks and spiffy tuxedoed turn in a television adaptation of And then There None, seemed to take himself right out of the next Bond sweepstakes in a Daily Mail interview. Turner, who is best known for the TV show Poldark, said that he was still able to go to pubs and travel on the tube in relative anonymity and that he'd be very reluctant to take on James Bond because this would change all of that. Turner wasn't too sure that he wanted the fame and attention which is part and parcel of Bond. This is exactly what troubled Daniel Craig back in 2005.

The premiere day for No Time to Die finally arrived. As one might expect it was a very glitzy and plush affair at the Royal Albert Hall. Magazine television shows in Britain were definitely in a Bond themed tizzy that day as they donned tuxedos and anticipated the spangled celebrity red carpet to come. The Prince of Wales, the Duchess of Cornwall, and the Duke and Duchess of Cambridge all attended the premiere. The cast of No Time to Die and Billie Eilish were present and celebrities who attended included Jason Momoa, Emma Raducanu, Harry Kane, Mo Farah and Stormzy. In a nice touch, Dame Judi Dench was also there - as was Michelle Yeoh. One other nice touch was that the producers had given free tickets to NHS staff and members of the British armed forces - two professions which had done vital work during the pandemic.

Phoebe Waller-Bridge was of course also present at the premiere. In the summer she had begun shooting her role in the fifth Indiana Jones film with Harrison Ford. Waller-Bridge was the female lead. Her character was described as an adventurer and a femme fatale. Shooting on Indiana Jones 5 was set to continue into the new year so Waller-Bridge was certainly busy. She had now enjoyed a brush with two genuine icons of the cinema. There was always the possibility too of Waller-Bridge turning up in a future Bond film in an acting (as opposed to writing) capacity. A Bond villain maybe?

Daniel Craig wore a red velvet jacket with black bow tie at the premiere and seemed more relieved than anything that the film was finally being screened. You could forgive him a degree of relief at the thought that his promotional duties as Bond were slowly but surely coming to an end. Interviewed on the red carpet, Craig confirmed yet again that this was definitely the end for him and that it was now time to move on as an actor. Craig was now 53 - the same age Sean Connery had been in Never Say Never Again. It was time to make way for a younger actor. Craig seemed happy and upbeat at the premiere. He joked in an interview for the NY Times at this time that he would probably be remembered as the 'grumpy' Bond but said he was fine with that. Craig was satisfied that he had put his own personal stamp on the character and done it his way. It would be left to existing and future Bond fans to argue over his retrospective legacy in the franchise.

Asked if he had any advice for his successor, Craig replied - "There's a couple things I'd say. One is don't be s***. I would say you have to grab it and make it your own. I hope I've left it in a good place and I hope the next person can just make it fly. It's an amazing franchise. I still think there's a lot of stories to tell." Daniel Craig was unique among Bond actors in that he had dictated the time and style of his departure. It was still hard to imagine that another Bond actor would enjoy so much influence again.

There was a slightly strange atmosphere at the premiere because social distancing was still in effect. As a consequence of this there was no media scrum or crowds of autograph hunters jostling for position next to the actors and celebrities. Anyone off-camera had to wear a mask. It was a beautiful day earlier in London but the skies darkened and drizzled during the premiere - prompting a fair amount of umbrellas to be deployed. One hoped the sudden deluge wasn't a metaphor for the movie! The entrance of the Royal Albert Hall was festooned with Bond props and music from the Craig Bond films blasted out from speakers. Even this slightly strange premiere though was still a happy event. It just a great relief to finally have the film released.

Jeffrey Wright sported a green tux while Lashana Lynch was resplendent in yellow. Léa Seydoux wore a silver dress that seemed to have a cape too. Ana de Armas stole the show by wearing a black dress which looked like the one she wore in the actual movie. Though her role in No Time to Die only amounted to several minutes of screentime, Ana de Armas would be equally scene stealing in the film too. The premiere was fun for fashion commentators but most Bond fans were not especially interested in the posh frocks and tuxedos. They were instead anticipating the fact that some reviews of the actual movie would soon be forthcoming. No Time to Die was also going to be screened for critics in other countries too on premiere day. The moment of truth had finally arrived. Would this film live up to all the marketing hype that had been bestowed on it for what seemed like forever?

It was pretty surreal, after all the delays and false starts, to think that we were finally about to find out if the film was all that it had been cracked up to be by EON during those endless promotional campaigns. "We have all missed the experience of going to the cinema not just for the story but also to be thrilled," said Cary Fukunaga onstage before the screening. "I am thrilled to be sharing the 25th James Bond the way it was meant to be seen: on the big screen." And with that, the film was shown for the invited audience.

The next day the reviews finally (FINALLY!) of No Time to Die began to tumble forth. The early reviews from British critics were so gushing that a stratospheric Skyfall style Rotten Tomatoes score seemed on the cards initially. Glowing reviews from a raft of publications followed - including a surprising 5/5 from The Guardian. The Guardian said the film had 'pathos, action, drama, camp comedy, heartbreak, macabre horror, and outrageously silly old-fashioned action'. The Telegraph was equally impressed and wrote - 'Cary Joji Fukunaga's extravagantly satisfying, bulgingly proportioned last chapter to the Craig era, throws almost everything there is left to throw at 007 the series can come up with'.

The BBC was also firmly in the praise camp and awarded No Time to Die five out of five stars. 'If there are other elements, too,' wrote the BBC, 'which don't quite reach the heights they're aiming for, in general No Time To Die does exactly what it was intended to do, which is to round off the Craig era with tremendous ambition and aplomb. Beyond that, it somehow succeeds in taking something from every single other Bond film, and sticking them all together. To quote a certain song that makes a wistful reappearance: if that's all we have, we need nothing more.'

Digital Spy also judged the film to be a worthy conclusion to the Craig era but opined that it didn't hit the heights of Casino Royale and Skyfall. The Independent was one of the few British newspapers to be lukewarm, writing - 'What's most disappointing is how strangely anti-climatic the whole thing feels. Despite Phoebe Waller-Bridge's much-publicised contributions to the film's script, No Time to Die hardly feels like the radical feminist rewrite we were promised.'

The first really negative review came from Screen International - which complained that the film lacked fun and wit. Forbes was also unimpressed and said the film was hamstrung by its determination to be a sequel to Spectre. Forbes also opined that the central romance in No Time to Die was not helped by the fact that the aged Daniel Craig looked more like his leading lady's father than her lover. The early reviews were, on the whole, overwhelmingly positive but enough nitpickers emerged in the end to knock the RT score down from the high 90s to the early 80s - which was still perfectly respectable.

Among those nitpickers was The AV Club, who wrote - 'No Time To Die is forgettable in all the places that usually count—it's a Bond movie with little excitement or panache. All the film has to distinguish it is an uncharacteristically sappy ending, a late bid to jerk some tears after nearly three hours of boring us to them.' 007 Magazine also disliked the film and called it 'flabby, overlong and unsatisfying'. 007 Magazine called No Time to Die's OHMSS riffs 'ersatz and second hand' and felt that the performances of Daniel Craig and Léa Seydoux existed in an 'emotional vacuum' and thus failed to sell the central romance upon which the movie had built its very foundations on.

Rex Reed of Observer also disliked the film. 'No Time to Die may not be the worst James Bond movie ever made, but it's in heavy competition as the dullest one since Octopussy. The film's sole distinction is the fact that it's the James Bond epic that finally manages to make 007 a crashing bore. Directed with more boyish slobber than narrative coherence by Cary Joji Fukunaga from an over-crammed, self-consciously contrived script by no fewer than five writers.' The negative reviews became more frequent when the American critics began posting their articles. You can generally expect a Bond film to get a fairly free ride in Britain (let's be honest, places like Empire and Total Film are never going to completely trash a Bond film they've just enjoyed privileged access and exclusives to!) but this is not the case in America - and rightly so.

The main criticisms of the movie from naysayers were that it was overlong (to be fair to Empire, their otherwise positive review DID complain that the movie was too long and bogged down by exposition in its middle act), too sentimental, and too gloomy and miserable. Generally though, the film got fairly good reviews on the whole. You wouldn't say that critics - as a whole - found it too divisive. This decidedly wouldn't be the case with Bond fans though. They WOULD find No Time to Die divisive. For those interested in such statistics, Metacritic assigned No Time to Die a weighted average score of 69 out of 100. The general feeling then, in terms of critic scores, was that No Time to Die fell short of Casino Royale and Skyfall but was stronger than Quantum of Solace and Spectre. This placed it squarely in the middle of the Craig era when it came to film critics.

With the premiere out of the way and EON doubtless reasonably happy with the reviews of the film that were flooding the online world, Daniel Craig, like a weary marathon runner with only one mile left to run, was wheeled around television studios and video feeds on both sides of the Atlantic in one more final publicity heave. Craig was definitely demob happy by this point. One got the impression that, just for a change, he was actually quite enjoying this Bond publicity drive because he knew he'd never have to do this again. Craig seemed to be enjoying his twilight days as Bond. All this media attention would instantly transfer over to his successor one day and Craig would then suddenly become another ex-Bond actor like Pierce Brosnan or Timothy Dalton. But for now, for this moment, he was still James Bond and still the centre of attention.

The rest of the No Time to Die cast also did their bit in this last promotional quest and Cary Fukunaga (who must have been one of the most interviewed people in the world in 2021) continued to conduct interviews like they were going out of fashion. If he was slightly bored of talking about No Time to Die by now Fukunaga displayed no sign of this. Like the rest of the Bond team he just seemed happy and relieved that the film had finally been released and seemed to have garnered a positive enough reception. In October, Daniel Craig and Rami Malek made a surprise appearance at an IMAX cinema in Burbank, California, and got up on stage introduce a screening of No Time to Die. Craig told the audience it was a great thrill to finally have the film in cinemas and being watched by the public.

No Time to Die had a $55.2 million opening in the United States - which was down on the more optimistic projections. It dropped 57% in its second week. The main competition in cinemas around this time were Halloween Kills and Dune. In the end, No Time to Die would gross around $160 million in North America. This was generally seen as a disappointment because Spectre and Skyfall had both grossed considerably more than that. It was hard to say if it was the lingering pandemic effect or American audiences getting a trifle bored of the Daniel Craig era of Bond. Maybe it was a bit of both.

The truth is though that, a few exceptions aside, Bond has

always made much of its money outside of the United States and is not entirely dependent on North America for revenue. It could be that the 163 minute running time of the film was a factor in that cinemas couldn't squeeze in as many screenings as they might have liked. No Time to Die ended up as the seventh highest grossing film of the year in the United States. Aside from F9: The Fast Saga, all the films that outgrossed No Time to Die were superhero movies.

There was much better news in Britain - where No Time to Die grossed incredible $96 million by the end of the year. This was on a par with Skyfall and Spectre - which was no mean feat given the strange circumstances in which the movie was released. No Time to Die's gross in Britain was quite incredible. Cinema owners in Britain breathed a heavy sigh of relief when these amazing numbers started tumbling in. They'd been banking on Bond to save them and this is exactly what had transpired.

MGM and EON (not to mention Universal - who were partners on this film and handled the American distribution) would also have been delighted to see No Time to Die become the highest grossing non-Chinese film of the year in China. The film also performed strongly in Europe and the Middle East. In most places around the world cinemagoers were clearly very happy to have the chance to go out and watch a new James Bond film again after the long wait and the difficult times they had endured. No Time to die was certainly raking in the money but it still remained uncertain if it would make enough to turn in a profit. The months ahead would answer that question.

* The praise which greeted Casino Royale in 2006 must have been noted with a wry smile by Timothy Dalton. In 2006, you might venture, they sort of embraced again what Dalton had tried to do with the character in the late 1980s. 'The globetrotting espionage antics of Dalton's 007 were depicted in a much more realistic manner than the average Bond plot,' wrote GamesRadar. 'Casino Royale would later be lauded for

grounding the Bond franchise in gritty realism, but the short-lived Dalton era already did that. Dalton's Bond acted on his own authority, following his own judgment, which resulted in more morally challenging stories than fans were accustomed to. Dalton did a lot of his own stunts – unlike Moore, whose stunt doubles could be spotted from a mile away – and his love interests had a lot more agency than the average Bond girls. None of the romantic scenes in Dalton's movies have the problematic overtones that most of the other movies do, because his Bond was actually interested in connecting with women instead of objectifying them.' Timothy Dalton has at least received some overdue credit for the changes he tried to implement on the Bond franchise. Dalton has always been appreciated in Bond fandom though. It would probably be reasonable to say that Timothy Dalton was always more appreciated by Bond fans than casual audiences.

# CHAPTER THREE - SHADOWS OF OHMSS

It won't have escaped Bond fans that No Time to Die is desperate to dredge up the emotional impact of OHMSS. To this end we get endless snippets of the Bond/Tracey love theme We Have all the Time in the World in the music score of the film. No Time to Die is quite blatant in its desperate desire to somehow connect itself to OHMSS. On Her Majesty's Secret Service was the eleventh James Bond novel written by Ian Fleming and first published in 1963. It begins with James Bond on leave in Royale-les-Eaux, unwinding on the continent and increasingly weary of his job, duty, and so far fruitless search for Blofeld in the operation to mop-up the remnants of SPECTRE. He makes a first draft of a letter of resignation to M and meets and falls in love with Contessa Teresa (Tracey) di Vicenzo after bailing her out at the Casino in Monte Carlo and preventing her from taking her own life.

Bond is then taken captive by Tracey's father Marc-Ange

Draco, head of a crime organization called The Union Corse - 'More deadly and perhaps even older than the Unione Siciliano, the Mafia...it controlled most organized crime throughout metropolitan France and her colonies.' Draco fears for his unstable daughter and offers Bond a million pounds if he will marry her. Bond declines this offer but he agrees to continue to see Tracey and watch over her if Draco will help him locate a certain Ernst Stavro Blofeld.

One of the most famous of the James Bond books - and one that duly made the best James Bond film - On Her Majesty's Secret Service is an enjoyable piece of escapism that takes a more human Bond on an adventure from France to the Swiss Alps with suspense, intrigue and some excellent snowy chase sequences. A classic adventure that pits Bond against Blofeld with the high stakes a potential biological threat to Great Britain - to be delivered in a very novel way. On Her Majesty's Secret Service also has a shocking twist (or two) in the colourful life of James Bond.

Ian Fleming's knack for vividly taking you to exotic places immediately draws you into On Her Majesty's Secret Service as Bond ambles around sunny France with bronzed girls drinking coffee in outdoor cafés and a gentle breeze in the air. It's quite interesting the way it captures Bond at a confused and low-ebb as he drafts a letter of resignation (which we can read in the book) and finds himself questioning his life and duty - 'He was fed up to the teeth with chasing the ghost of Blofeld. And the same went for SPECTRE. The thing had been smashed. Even a man of Blofeld's genius, in the impossible event that he still existed, could never get a machine of that calibre running again.'

Bond being Bond, he becomes intrigued by Tracey after she overtakes him on a stretch of road - 'If there was one thing that set James Bond really moving, it was being passed at speed by a pretty girl.' Tracey ('Teresa was a saint, I am not a saint') is one of the most complex and memorable of Fleming's Bond girls with crucial role in the story and indeed James Bond's life. The early casino scenes are very stylish and generate a lot of tension as Tracey, who is in the grip of 'some deep melancholy, some form of spiritual accidie' recklessly gambles with no credit. You do find yourself becoming immediately interested in Tracey's welfare and eccentricity and want to find out more about her just like Bond.

Although Tracey leaves the narrative for a while she is firmly established - 'She had come from nowhere and was standing behind the croupier, and Bond had no time to take in more than golden arms, a beautiful golden face with brilliant blue eyes.' Bond knows that Tracey will be blacklisted which Fleming tells us is a bit like being declared a bad risk at Lloyds. Tracey will be a social leper in these swanky circles. 'In American gambling circles, she might even have been liquidated.' As ever we get to know a little more about Bond and these titbits are always enjoyable. In On Her Majesty's Secret Service we learn that Bond returns to the grave of Vesper Lynd each year, had a Swiss mother, and, unlike M, is a fan of Rex Stout's Nero Wolfe mysteries.

The book has some great locations including M's country residence Quarterdeck and Piz Gloria, Blofeld's mountain retreat - 'Below, the ground was mostly in darkness, but ahead giant peaks were still golden in the dying sun. They were making straight for one of them, for a small plateau near its summit. A cable car, spangled in the sun, was creeping down.' Blofeld has a weird mountain sanatorium where he is treating young women suffering from allergies and there is a surprising amount of tension when Bond goes undercover there posing as Sir Hilary Bray from the Royal College of Arms. Bond must hide his identity while seeking information and you do feel the danger of his situation. Blofeld contacted the College to establish a family connection to the de Bleuville title and the British government were tipped off accordingly.

The battle of wits between Blofeld (who has undergone plastic surgery) and Bond is very absorbing and there are some great action sequences in this inventive alpine location. In addition to Blofeld and Tracey, Fleming gives us another memorable character here in Irma Blunt, Blofeld's factotum/assistant. On Her Majesty's Secret Service is a very enjoyable James Bond novel with an entertaining story and some dark twists. It is essentially the second part of the 'Blofeld' trilogy, following on from Thunderball and part of a story arc continued in You Only Live Twice.

Fleming's OHMSS benefited greatly from the fact that in the Broccoli/Saltzman movie franchise it was one of the few books to get a fairly faithful screen adaptation. Imagine for a moment now that you are EON in 1968. You are sitting on a goldmine, otherwise known as the James Bond series, but a certain Sean Connery has departed. You want to make more James Bond films but with who? Who can replace Connery? A big Hollywood star? Should the character remain in the Connery style or be changed?

You probably can't win whatever you do, but if you want to make another James Bond film you need a new James Bond actor. We are probably all familiar now with the story of how a young Australian living in London blagged his way to a screentest and broke stuntman Yuri Borienko's nose shooting test footage. While there were several respected actors involved in the OHMSS casting call, none had the Bond 'look' quite like George Lazenby. * He was physical, young and looked just like James Bond. Could his non-existent acting experience be countered and hidden by a crafty director? The director Peter Hunt thought so.

The pre-credit sequence in the film version of OHMSS is a bit of a tease at first. After a brief scene with M and Q, Moneypenny is asked by M if she knows the whereabouts of 007. The Bond music strikes up and we see the famous Aston Martin. Bond is following a red sportscar along a coastal road but we don't see him immediately. The new James Bond is glimpsed only in shadow. 007 has been tailing Countess Tracy di Vicenzo (played by Diana Rigg as if you didn't know).

Tracey stops her car, gets out and starts walking into the sea in a glittering dress. John Barry's atmospheric music fits perfectly. Bond jumps out of his car and runs out to sea to rescue her. After a "My name's Bond, James Bond" (where we get our first proper look at Lazenby) we see that a bunch of goons have surrounded Bond and Tracey. The fight sequence that follows shows exactly why they cast Lazenby. This man can look after himself. Lazenby's energy and willingness to throw himself into the fight scenes is very evident. I don't think the "This never happened to the other fella" line was completely necessary but it was a nod to the fact that Connery was gone before, seconds later, we see the hands of time being pulled back at the beginning of the title sequence to signify a new beginning.

The title sequence by Maurice Binder is excellent. An instrumental version of John Barry's OHMSS theme plays over film of characters from the previous Bond films. The link to the past reminds us that this is still James Bond - despite a change of actor. Barry's theme is inspired and if you don't own it already you get should hold of Propellerheads' remix. At the start of the film Bond pulls into a hotel and inquires about the Red Cougar parked outside. The car belongs to Tracey and they meet again at the casino where Bond bails her out after she makes a risky bet that she can't pay.

The casino scenes in OHMSS look very lavish and expensive. Lazenby isn't entirely comfortable in his first casino scenes with Rigg but he is more effective when they go upstairs and Tracey threatens to kill him for a 'thrill'. He has another brutal punch-up ("Gatecrasher!") and once again we are reminded why Lazenby got the job. No other Bond actor can scrap as convincingly as Lazenby. Bond wakes to find Tracey has gone although she has paid her debt in full. Off for a game of golf, 007 has a gun pointed at him in the Hotel lobby and is kidnapped by several shady looking characters.

They take him to an abandoned dockside warehouse. A cleaner whistles a few notes from Goldfinger as they enter and note how Lazenby pushes the mini door behind him so it hits the goon behind. A simple but effective moment. We then get yet another Lazenby punch-up with great OTT sound-effects. I disagree with people who say that the fights in OHMSS are too fast and over-edited. I think they're great!

We meet Marc-Ange Draco (a dubbed Gabriele Ferzetti). Tracey is Draco's daughter and he wants Bond to marry her. According to Draco she needs a man to dominate her. I'm not sure you could get away with that line today! Draco tells Bond that he will pay him one million pounds sterling on the day that he marries Tracey. Bond tells Draco that he doesn't need a million pounds or a wife, although he admits to a fascination with Tracey ("I find her fascinating but, she needs a psychiatrist, not me.") This is one scene that slows the film down a bit but it is a crucial one. It sets up the motivation of Bond and Draco and introduces Blofeld into the plot.

Draco has an ace up his sleeve. He can find Ernst Stavro Blofeld. Bond is desperate for this information and agrees to see Tracey again. Back at Universal Exports, 007 is furious when M informs him he is to be taken off the Blofeld case. He resigns in the form of a letter dictated to Moneypenny. "Same old James...only more so!" says Moneypenny in another reference to the cheeky new Bond. 007 then sits in his office and raises his hip flask to a portrait of the Queen. He takes props from previous Bond films from his desk and we hear the music from each film. This is a wonderful moment. As too is the next scene where Bond discovers that Moneypenny has changed his letter from one of resignation to a request for some time off. Both M and Bond are relieved at the outcome and we see how important Moneypenny is to both of them.

In Portugal Bond is confronted by Tracey. Tracey has discovered the deal between Bond and Draco and demands that Bond should receive his information and leave. 007 chooses to stay and becomes closer to Tracey. The musical montage with 'We Have All The Time In The World' is another classic moment. The romance is developed in OHMSS and not compressed. This means we feel more empathy for Bond and Tracey. The safe-cracking sequence (absent from British television prints for years) is another classic slice of sixties Bond. Lazenby is very cool as he flips through a copy of Playboy and then leaves in a very laid back almost Connery like manner.

Blofeld is attempting to lay claim to the title 'Comte Balthazar de Bleuchamp'. This angle fits in with the casting of Telly Savalas - who isn't as aristocratic as other Blofeld actors. This Blofeld is like a gangster who is desperate to be sophisticated. Bond is put in contact with Sir Hilary Bray (George Baker) at the College Of Arms in London. M gives Bond permission to pose as Sir Hilary and visit Blofeld's mountain top clinic in Switzerland. Was there ever a cooler or more spectacular location in the Bond series than Piz Gloria? Blofeld has set up a clinical research institute at Piz Gloria where a number of young women are being treated for allergies and phobias. In reality the girls have been brainwashed and can be used as Blofeld's agents to spread his (Infertility) Virus Omega into the world.

The helicopter ride up to Piz Gloria ** is another illustration of the scope of the film. It really does look glorious. Blofeld does not recognise Bond - despite their meeting in the last film. Continuity was never rigid in the old series so it doesn't really bother one anyway. I like the Sir Hilary section a great deal and we get a few choice double-entendres as Bond starts seducing the patients to gain information. Lazenby (much to his annoyance when he found out) is dubbed for this part of the film by George Baker. Angela Scoular is fun as Ruby Bartlett and you may spot a young Joanna Lumley among the girls.

Bond is eventually rumbled. "No no no, Mr. Bond. Respectable baronets from the College of Heralds do NOT seduce female patients in clinics!" says Blofeld. He has a point I think! Bond escapes and we have the first classic ski chase in the franchise. From here on in OHMSS is action-packed and as good as a

Bond film can get. 007 seeks refuge in the snowy village below where a festival is in full swing and, after a loud fight in a shed full of bells, he moves through the crowds aware that Blofeld's men are moving in on him. He sits by the skating rink and appears to be out of ideas and places to run. The skaters whirl around the edge of the rink and flash past. Suddenly one stops abruptly in front of 007. The camera pans up and we see Diana Rigg as Tracey! A classic moment.

They take Tracey's car and we have one of the most exciting sections of the series as they try to escape. Eventually they gatecrash a stockcar race on ice! "Looks like we've hit the rushhour!" says Bond. John Barry's music is the perfect background to this section of the film. Bond and Tracey spend the night in an old barn as a blizzard rattles the doors outside. 007 decides to quit MI6 and marry Tracey. After another great ski chase Tracey is captured by Blofeld and Bond is presumed dead in an avalanche created by Blofeld. Back in London Bond stares out of the window lost in thought and an image of an unconscious Tracey being dragged out of the snow is projected on the window. OHMSS is full of great little moments like this. I love the sweep of Barry's music when, earlier in the film, Bond's car enters the grounds of M's home.

Bond is told to keep his beak out by M but he enlists Draco's help. "I'd like to interest you in a demolition deal that requires certain aerial activity to install equipment." The great thing about the classic Bonds is the BIG ending. The spectacular battle scenes with Bond in the middle of the action. OHMSS is hard to beat for this. We have alpine soldiers, explosions, flamethrowers. Bond chases Blofeld through a lab bathed in psychedelic colours. Lazenby is every inch James Bond here. Bond and Blofeld end up having a bobsleigh chase in what seems like the third or fourth climax to the film. In OHMSS Bond is more human and uses less gadgets but the film is as action-packed as any in the series.

The downbeat ending was a brave move and Lazenby deserves much credit for the way he handles the scene. You couldn't imagine Connery's Bond as a broken man like Lazenby is here. Lazenby's basic acting range and youth work in his favour a lot in OHMSS. It's a shame that people who have probably never even sat through OHMSS probably think he was terrible. Diana Rigg's casting in the film was an inspired move. She is head and shoulders above the other Bond women and I like Telly Savalas too as a different sort of Blofeld. How would I sum up On Her Majesty's Secret Service? The best James Bond film ever made!

In 2013, the film director Steven Soderbergh went into bat for OHMSS and argued this very case when he said - "Shot to shot, this movie is beautiful in a way none of the other Bond films are — the anamorphic compositions are relentlessly arresting — and the editing patterns of the action sequences are totally bananas; it's like Peter Hunt took all the ideas of the French new wave and blended them with Eisenstein in a Cuisinart to create a grammar that still tops today's how fast can you cut aesthetic, because the difference here is that each of the shots — no matter how short — are real shots, not just additional coverage from the hosing-it-down school of action, so there is a unification of the aesthetic of the first unit and the second unit that doesn't exist in any other Bond film. And, speaking of action, there are as many big set pieces in OHMSS as any Bond film ever made, and if that weren't enough, there's a great score by John Barry, some really striking sound work, and what can you say about Diana Rigg that doesn't start with the word WOW?"

The interesting thing about On Her Majesty's Secret Service is that it showed the Bond formula was more flexible than might have been suspected. Compared to gargantuan tongue-in-cheek extravaganzas like Thunderball and You Only Live Twice, OHMSS was surprisingly dramatic and emotional. It presented Bond not as an indestructible superhero but as someone who could have his heart broken. OHMSS was the first film in the franchise that explored the concept of making Bond more human. It was this film which paved the way for Timothy Dalton and Daniel Craig to present what you might describe as less flippant versions of the character in the future.

The main problem with No Time to Die's frequent references to OHMSS is that we are simply reminded that OHMSS is a better film. Presumably, the No Time to Die filmmakers and composer figured that most casual viewers have probably never even sat through OHMSS and wouldn't even get the reference anyway. Bond films have occasionally recycled music before (you can detect some of the techno remix for John Barry's OHMSS theme during the Hamburg car park chase in Tomorrow Never Dies) but the use of the love theme from OHMSS in No Time to Die is more blatant. It's as if they thought they could somehow transplant the romantic spirit of OHMSS into their movie simply by lifting some of the music. No Time to Die also borrows the biological villain caper of OHMSS.

Though the lazy general perception of OHMSS is that it was the oddity with the Australian fellow that bombed, Bond fans (well, most of them, I'm sure there are Bond fans who don't like OHMSS and prefer other movies in the franchise) are well aware that OHMSS is actually a terrific and very stylish film. Cary Fukunaga named OHMSS as his favourite Bond film (alongside Casino Royale) during interviews for No Time to Die. This might partly explain why No Time to Die is so desperate to hitch its wagon to OHMSS and somehow connect itself to that movie. What they didn't seem to understand though is that OHMSS is not a 'serious' movie. It does not wallow in melodrama or have an inflated sense of its own importance in the same manner that you might argue No Time to Die does.

In fact, OHMSS is for the most part a briskly paced 007 romp. It has bags of action, a villain with a mountain top base, humour, casinos, car chases, ski chases, and gadgets. Lazenby's Bond in OHMSS is not miserable or tortured. He gambles, beats people up, dispenses quips, and seduces several women. Lazenby's Bond, until the end, is having a pretty good time in OHMSS. He clearly enjoys his job. It is only at the conclusion of the film, after Bond has fallen in love with Tracey and is therefore now vulnerable, that we get the emotional gut punch of Tracey's death - which leaves Bond broken. That amounts to a minute or so of the film. No Time to Die, by contrast, often feels like it is trying to present us with a 'broken Bond' for most of its running time! In the next chapter we will assess how successful this strategy turned out to be.

* George Lazenby said he only got the part of James Bond about two weeks before shooting was due to commence for On Her Majesty's Secret Service. Lazenby, unless you count a Big Fry chocolate commercial, wasn't even an actor when he became James Bond. He had rather blagged his way to an audition by pretending to be a playboy and actor. "I had no acting experience," said Lazenby. "I was coming from the male model point of view. I walked in looking like James Bond, and acting as if that's the way I was anyway. And they thought, 'All we have to do is keep this guy just the way he is and we'll have James Bond.'" Lazenby went to a voice trainer before he auditioned for Bond in an attempt to tone down his Australian accent. Lazenby was up against John Richardson, Hans de Vries, Robert Campbell and Anthony Rogers in the final James Bond auditions for On Her Majesty's Secret Service. John Richardson turned out to be his closest rival. Richardson had starred in fairly big films like One Million Years B.C. and She for Hammer.

On the first day of shooting for On Her Majesty's Secret Service, a security guard on the gate at Pinewood Studios didn't recognise George Lazenby and wouldn't let him in. That turned out to be a portent of things to come. George Lazenby and director Peter Hunt fell out during the production of On Her Majesty's Secret Service. Lazenby said that they barely spoke to each other for much of the shoot. Lazenby said he found Diana Rigg a bit snooty on the set of On Her Majesty's Secret Service. Lazenby said that Rigg seemed to think she was the star of the film (in fairness to Diana Rigg she was a much bigger name than Lazenby and a vastly more experienced and talented thespian). If rumours are to believed though, they had a brief affair making this movie.

The news that George Lazenby had probably quit the Bond franchise leaked before On Her Majesty's Secret Service was released. As a consequence, the promotional campaign downplayed Lazenby and billed James Bond as the star. This was very different from the Connery films - which also made a big deal of declaring that Sean Connery IS James Bond. Cubby Broccoli told George Lazenby not to come to the On Her Majesty's Secret Service premiere looking scruffy. You can probably guess what happened. Lazenby, ever the rebel, turned up with long hair and a beard.

The most remarkable thing about Lazenby's departure from Bond is that he genuinely seemed to believe he was leaving a sinking ship. His agent Ronan O'Rahilly told him that James Bond was conservative and out of vogue. A dust shrouded relic of the fifties that would wheeze on for a couple more films and then be consigned to cinematic history. It was one of the stupidest pieces of advice anyone could ever be unfortunate enough to receive. Peter Hunt felt that George Lazenby would have made a great Bond if he'd stuck with the franchise. "Had George Lazenby been more sensible, and had Broccoli and Saltzman been more sensible with him, I think he would have made a very credible Bond. He was a great looking guy and he moved along very well, although he wasn't really an actor. He was a model who had not done any acting before that. I think if things had gone the other way, he would have gone on to be a very good Bond."

Lazenby is by far the worst paid Bond actor. Adjusted for inflation in today's money, Lazenby was paid about $400,000 for On Her Majesty's Secret Service. This made his decision to walk away from Bond after one film even more crazy. He should have done a couple more Bond films and then at least he could have walked away with a few million in the bank. George Lazenby said that, in hindsight, he had been very stupid by walking away from Bond after one movie. Lazenby noted that Connery was shrewd in that he only quit Bond after he had made plenty of money from it. Lazenby was foolish enough to quit Bond before it made him rich!

Lazenby claimed that after he quit the Bond franchise, Cubby Broccoli used his influence to have him shunned in the film industry. It's obviously impossible to verify these allegations. Lazenby's acting career (not that he had an acting career apart from OHMSS) after Bond did fall off a cliff though. A few years after OHMSS he was reduced to doing cheapjack kung fu films for peanuts in Hong Kong. Lazenby was pretty lucky though in that he apparently made a lot of money from real estate. His aptitude for business meant he didn't have to rely on acting to earn a living - which is probably just as well given how his acting career turned out.

** In early plans for the film adaptation of On Her Majesty's Secret Service, Blofeld's headquarters was going to be located on the Maginot Line. The Maginot Line was a series of fortifications built by the French in the 1930s to protect themselves from any German aggression. It was manned by the French army and even had its own subway system. It proved to be ineffective in World War 2 because the Germans aimed the focal point of their attack at the Ardennes region of Belgium and simply bypassed the Maginot Line. After the war ended, French troops were stationed at the Maginot Line again and one of its biggest bunkers became a NATO command centre. When France left NATO in 1966, the Maginot Line was abandoned.

# CHAPTER FOUR - NO TIME TO DIE

No Time to Die's release finally allowed us to see how many of the endless rumours and also alleged leaks in the previous months were true or not. It turned out that most of them were indeed true. The pre-credit sequence really did turn out to be unusually long. Bond did indeed turn out to have a child. Many characters were indeed killed off. Most surprising of all though - and something that we probably didn't expect - was the fact that James Bond was among the characters who shuffled off this mortal fictional coil by the time the end credits rolled. This would turn out to be a divisive creative decision among Bond fans to put it mildly. The controversy over making Bond and Blofeld step-brothers in Spectre was a storm in a teacup by comparison. One thing we can say about the Craig era is that it definitely loved killing people off. Even Judi Dench's dear old M was bumped off in Skyfall. Felix Leiter was another character to bite the dust in No Time to Die and he was followed by Blofeld. If they'd blown up Q and Moneypenny too you probably wouldn't have been surprised. No Time to Die was that sort of film. It really was the end of something.

It would be probably be generally fair (and rather predictable) to say that if you loved the Daniel Craig era so far you probably liked No Time to Die. If you were tired of the Daniel Craig era or never liked it much in the first place then bad luck because you probably didn't enjoy No Time to Die. No Time to Die doubles down on the backstory and maudlin melodrama of the Craig era more than ever. No Time to Die is an unashamedly undiluted Craig era film. All the stuff you either love or hate in the Craig era is here in spades. Backstory, melodrama, Bond as a reluctant spy, Bourne inspired fights and action scenes, Bond retired, Madeleine Swann, more melodrama, Bond depressed, and so on. There are though, despite this, surprisingly, still some strange tensions when it comes to the tone in No Time to Die.

Some sections of the film are overwrought and angsty and then you are occasionally and suddenly thrown into a fight or quip that could have come straight out of a Brosnan or Roger Moore film. No Time to Die is resolute in its determination to give Craig a 'drama' but is not immune to reaching up and plucking a more flippant trope from the 007 back catalogue. Stylistically, the film doesn't feel drastically different from the Sam Mendes films which preceded it. In terms of its narrative decisions though No Time to Die is what you might describe as bold and unusual. As the full stop to a 'miniseries within the series' No Time to Die is plainly not constrained by any conventional rules. The Bond formula is assuredly not set in stone here. How about Bond finds out he has a kid? Fine, throw it in there. How about we blow Bond to smithereens at the end? Sure, why not? Why don't we kill Felix too? Fine, let's drown him!

The film begins with a gunbarrel intro (a rarity in the Craig films!) which dispenses with the traditional blood flowing down the screen. It has been theorised that the bloodless gunbarrel signifies in No Time to Die that Bond has finally missed his target and thus has a subtext which anticipates Bond's death. If you believe this theory then the bloodless gunbarrel is visual shadowing that Bond could die in this film. The theme of No Time to Die is that James Bond (specifically Craig's version of Bond - obviously) was always doomed. 00 agents, as we were reminded in 2006's Casino Royale, do not have a long life expectancy. In the Fleming novels, OO agents must retire from active service at the age of 45. James Bond didn't expect to live this long anyway. Bond has killed many people and those who live by the sword must die by the sword. Bond sacrifices his life in No Time to Die to protect the family he will never know. He was briefly allowed to glimpse the happiness and alternative life denied to him.

After the gunbarrel there is an extended sequence where Lyutsifer Safin (Malek) stalks the young Madeleine Swann through an ice frosted Norwegian lake after murdering her mother. This is revenge for the fact that Mr White (on the orders of Blofeld) murdered Safin's family. You could forgive Bond fans if they suddenly feel like they need a refresher course on Madeleine and Mr White at this stage. We are expected to remember a lot about the previous Craig films to truly understand No Time to Die. Whether or not this interconnected approach was the right strategy is, as we have discussed, really all down to one's personal taste in the end.

Some of us were perfectly happy with stand alone adventures but it's perfectly fine also to desire more continuity within a particular era of the franchise. One can't help feeling though that Craig's era did end up with a sense that they were making it up as as they went along rather than adhering to a coherent long term narrative plan. You can see the consequences of not having a coherent plan in place for a connected movie cycle in films like Star Wars: The Rise of Skywalker. No Time to Die's problems are not as bad as that movie because the Craig era is not connective to the same degree that a Star Wars trilogy needs to be but you still tend to get the impression that the connected theme of the Daniel Craig Bond films was something that they stumbled into by accident and gamely juggled as they went along rather than something they meticulously planned from the get go.

The sequence with Safin and the young Madeleine in Norway which begins No Time to Die is stylish and creepy. Cary Fukunaga is able to both flex some of his horror movie chops (lest we forget, he was the original director of the big screen adaptation of Stephen King's IT but left due to creative differences) and also deconstruct the assumed formula of James Bond. We expect Bond films to begin with a stunt involving Bond * but No Time to Die does something completely different. This is one sequence in the film where all the hype concerning how we should expect the unexpected in No Time to Die lives up to its billing. The Safin depicted in this opening scene also more than lives up to the marketing hype EON had bestowed on their villain in the various aborted promotional campaigns leading up to the film. Safin seems sinister, unfathomable, scary, and downright weird in this opening sequence. He's basically a horror film villain in this sequence - and that works just fine.

This all sadly turns out to be something of a false dawn because Safin, as a character, is nowhere near as effective again in the (very long) film that follows. Not only is Safin underused in No Time to Die (which seems strange given the coup of landing Rami Malek in the first place and the months of hype over his participation) he is also curiously dull when he turns up again later in the film. Though he is supposed to be driving the plot and tension, Safin doesn't seem to have any impact as a character in the back half of No Time to Die. He just feels like a generic underwritten Bond villain of the type that is easily forgotten. A big problem is that Safin's motivation in No Time to Die is rather vague. This is what you could describe as an undercooked movie villain. It seems that neither the script nor Rami Malek ever quite managed to get a grasp on Safin and work out exactly what this villain is supposed to be or even what he is supposed to be doing in the film.

This is a shame really as anticipation for Malek's villain was very high after all the marketing hoopla. Do you remember how Barbara Broccoli said that Safin was someone who really got under Bond's skin? The connection and eventual duel between Bond and Safin turns out to disappointingly unaffecting and underwritten in No Time to Die. Safin talks in a silly foreign accent and kidnaps people. His biological doomsday shenanigans feel like something we've already seen in Bond films before - and more than once. The villain in this film is no Auric Goldfinger or Red Grant that's for sure.

'Safin isn't really a character,' wrote themovieblog.com. 'His motivations are murky and hazy. He seems like a collection of tropes loosely assembled in the shape of a Bond villain: he has a facial disfigurement, he has a cool isolated island base, he has colourful henchmen, he has a genocidal plan seemingly for the sake of it. This is one of the big problems with No Time to Die. So much of the movie is anchored in a very specific and very personal motivation for Safin, with his obvious reasons for dismantling SPECTRE. However, the film's last hour requires a pivot towards world domination that isn't really explained or articulated.'

The rumours that Safin was really Dr No turn out to be, as we all probably suspected, false in No Time to Die. Safin is definitely not Dr No - despite some snazzy sets which deliberately evoke the first Bond movie. Safin's costumes do take some inspiration from that first Bond villain too. You could argue a reasonable case that Blofeld should have been the main villain in No Time to Die rather than Safin. It feels anti-climatic to bring Blofeld back into the fold for No Time to Die and then do absolutely nothing with him at all. The device of making Blofeld some grand puppetmaster pulling all of these (retrospective) strings in the back end of Craig's tenure doesn't really work because it makes the villain seem second hand and offstage (which he largely is in No Time to Die - Waltz is only given one underwhelming scene). It breaks the rule of show don't tell.

After the Norway sequence which opens the film, No Time to Die then moves to Matera. Bond and (the now obviously adult) Madeleine Swann are (ahem) swanning around this lovely location in very James Bondish fashion. This part of the film feels the most like a Bond movie. It has the most Bond 'bumps' - as Cubby Broccoli would say. You have beautiful locations and the Aston Martin. The film wallows in Bond glamour and even Bond residue. Bond himself has yet to become embittered or depressed - as he soon shall in No Time to Die. Bond actually seems happy in these early scenes - which is certainly a rarity in this film.

Already though, the lack of romantic or sexual chemistry between Daniel Craig and Léa Seydoux is painfully apparent. Though he has been generally praised for his performances as Bond you could plausibly argue that this was a problem throughout the Craig Bond films. He rarely seemed to have much spark or chemistry with his leading ladies. Craig's Bond was quite chaste at times compared to the other Bonds and this theme continues in No Time to Die. Daniel Craig is the 'booziest' Bond in that his version of the character is seen drinking alcohol more often than the others. Craig's Bond knocks back plenty of sauce again in No Time to Die. On average, the cinematic Bond has a drink every 10 minutes, 53 seconds. Craig's Bond definitely lowered those numbers down a bit!

The Daniel Craig era was probably too reliant in the end on

Italian locations and the Aston Martin but you can forgive them for falling back on these Craig staples for this last final whirl around on the merry go round. They should seriously think about giving the next Bond actor a completely different car though to distinguish him from Craig - sort of like how they gave Roger Moore a Lotus to distinguish him from Sean Connery's Aston Martin driving 007. James Bond drives a Bentley in the Fleming novels. This car appeared in the film From Russia With Love.

Regarding the introduction of Bond's Aston Martin into the movie franchise, production designer Ken Adam said - "I had an E-type Jaguar in the 60s and I remember the debate about which sports car Bond should drive. We decided on the sexiest British sports car at the time and John Stears from special effects and myself went to Newport Pagnall, where they made Aston Martins, and they weren't at all helpful. Reluctantly, after the big boys from the studio stepped in, they let us have two, but after the Bond film their sales went up by 47% and there were no problems getting cars after that. I never owned one myself - if I remember correctly the clutch wasn't all that good."

Oddly, Daniel Craig's hair seems to be reddish brown in these early No Time to Die scenes but then blondish silver thereafter. Did they make an attempt to dye his hair and then forget about it? It's a strange little detail. Bond is persuaded to visit the grave of Vesper Lynd (yet another character cinemagoers are required to remember - though she is probably harder to forget than Madeleine as Casino Royale was much better received than Spectre and Vesper is a more memorable character than Madeleine) but her tomb explodes and Bond then barely survives numerous attempts to kill him. Bond visiting Vesper's grave is another OHMSS riff. In the novel On Her Majesty's Secret Service we learn that Bond visits the grave of Vesper Lynd once a year. Krystyna Skarbek, an agent Ian Fleming met during the war, was the inspiration for Vesper Lynd.

Much of the action we saw in the trailers comes from this extended early section of the movie. The Aston Martin machine gun sequence is great but its impact is somewhat lessened by the fact that we feel like we've already seen much of this scene before in the many promos and teasers. Even at this early stage in the film, Craig's Bond has already tilted into maudlin self-pity. He believes Madeleine has betrayed him. At one point, Bond even seems to consider doing nothing and allowing the baddies to simply shoot up the Aston Martin. He is practically suicidal. It will transpire that it was Blofeld who cooked up this bomb plot merely to make it look as if Bond had been betrayed. This does beg a rather obvious question. Why was Bond not able to deduce all of this for himself? This plot device doesn't make Craig's Bond seem very bright in the old brains department.

Bond swiftly packs Madeleine away on a train and washes his hands of her. The script is desperately hoping that we are deeply and emotionally effected by the sight of these lovers enduring a parting of the ways. Even at this very early stage of the film the script has gone all in on the assumption that we deeply care about the relationship between Bond and Madeleine and that this will provide the film with not only some touching drama but also some serious emotional heft. That would appear to have been a very risky gambit. Daniel Craig and Léa Seydoux don't have any detectable chemistry together as actors so the movie sets itself an almost impossible challenge in trying to make the considerable focus on this love story justify its own existence.

Madeleine Swann, ultimately, just isn't a very interesting character. Léa Seydoux is a fantastic actor in other things but for some reason she just doesn't register in Spectre and No Time to Die. She seems bland. It doesn't help that Madeleine's main function is to just look sad or tearful. This doesn't give Seydoux much to play and so she comes across as one-note and mopey. The frustrating thing is that Léa Seydoux is capable of much more than this but is constricted by the way her character is written. Seydoux is never given a chance to be witty or kick some ass like Diana Rigg was in OHMSS. Madeleine fades in the memory almost as soon as the film is over.

The title sequence by Daniel Kleinman is typically stylish although the mumbled theme song by Billie Eilish - despite the endless awards it was bewilderingly showered with - fails to have much impact or drama and feels oddly disconnected from the familiar Bond imagery. The theme songs written and chosen for the Daniel Craig era have largely been a very uninspiring bunch. In fact, if you discount k.d. lang's Surrender (which SHOULD have been the theme song for Tomorrow Never Dies but was relegated to the end titles in favour of a much weaker song performed by Sheryl Crow), we probably haven't had a great Bond song since 1989's Licence to Kill.

The title sequence to No Time to Die deliberately evokes the OHMSS titles with its use of ticking clock hands, an hourglass, and trident and shield Britannia imagery. There is a reference to Dr No too with the dots that herald the beginning of the titles. Daniel Kleinman is definitely one person who should be retained for the next era of Bond. He has proved to be a more than worthy successor to the great Maurice Binder. The titles cut to a high tech sequence in London where agents connected to Safin kidnap MI6 scientist Valdo Obruchev (David Dencik - who shamelessly mugs his comic relief supporting role) from a lab. British viewers may be mildly amused at this point to see sitcom star Hugh Dennis as one of the scientists. This skyscraper espionage feels like a lot like a hangover from that time when the Craig era was very inspired by Nolan's Batman films.

Safin's goons steal Project Heracles (Heracles was a divine hero in Greek mythology, the son of Zeus and Alcmene, and the foster son of Amphitryon) in their raid on the MI6 lab. Heracles is a biological weapon in which nanobots spread through skin. As you might imagine, this raid is an embarrassment to M. This biological weapon will ultimately lead to Bond's death. There is a deliberate irony in Bond being doomed by a virus created by the country that he has so loyally served. The subtext of this connection is that Bond was dead as soon as he became an MI6 agent. His line of work was too dangerous to expect a happy ending.

The nanobot McGuffin feels like something out of Die Another Day and adds a curiously fantastical element to a film which is ostensibly doing its best to be a (melo)drama. These elements do lead to a mild case of tonal whiplash at times. No Time to Die, if you strip it down, actually has a similar plot to Moonraker (the film not the book). The film occasionally has the air of a Frankenstein's monster Bond film where they are plucking all these little bits and pieces from other 007 movies. The music by Hans Zimmer in No Time to Die is rather disappointing and strangely forgettable. The cinematography by Linus Sandgren is certainly deserving of the highest praise though.

It is some years later in the film after the PTS and Bond, meanwhile, is now retired and living in Jamaica. The home of Ian Fleming. Fleming would rattle off the Bond books on a gold plated typewriter by the beach at his Goldeneye home. The reflective tone that entered the later Bond novels echoed Fleming's own increasing sense of mortality. He drank too much and smoked too much and was far too fond of rich luxury foods, meats and butter, suffering increasing heart problems. Fleming's death was hastened by the complex and knotty Thunderball court case he became embroiled in with Kevin McClory. You almost (but not quite perhaps) suspect that the Bond in No Time to Die is deliberately given a late Fleming subtext. Both feel tired and on borrowed time.

There is no avoiding the fact that No Time to Die at this point has a plot that we can't help feeling as if we've seen before. Bond was depressed and retired in Skyfall too. In fact, Craig's Bond seems to have spent most of his tenure as Bond retiring, going rogue, being presumed dead, or merely whittling time away as a drunken barfly! You can understand why some Bond fans would prefer it if Bond in the movies was just an MI6 agent who went on exciting exotic missions. Craig's Bond must have retired more times than Sugar Ray Leonard. Bond is visited by Felix Leiter. Leiter has a mission for Bond. He wants Bond to go and extract Obruchev from Cuba. This then was the mysterious 'package' that was teased in the cryptic synopsis for the film when shooting began.

Why the CIA would need to rely on a retired depressed British agent for an important mission is somewhat vague but then Bond's off the grid status and experience is definitely a plus as far as they are concerned. We could venture that it was Felix who insisted on Bond for this mission. Felix trusts Bond and considers him a friend. Maybe Felix thought this would be a good way to shake Bond out of his rut. It is nice to see Jeffrey Wright back in the franchise although he isn't given an awful lot to do in No Time to Die. Daniel Craig doesn't have much chemistry with Léa Seydoux or Lashana Lynch in No Time to Die but at least he does have a nice relaxed rapport with Jeffrey Wright.

One Bond trope that is absent in No Time to Die is gambling. One suspects that because of the heavy emphasis on gambling in Casino Royale they decided to give this a wide berth for the rest of the Craig era - which is probably fair enough. Daniel Craig slips back into the role of Bond reasonably well in No Time to Die. He has clearly aged since Spectre but acknowledges this in his performance. This is a weary and tired Bond. Craig does still have a tendency to overact though in places. One such moment comes when Bond meets Blofeld. Craig also overacts a bit when he has his big confrontation with Safin. Craig is determined to make these scenes feel like they have great weight and importance but it's a Bond film not Chekhov. As a consequence of this there are scenes in No Time to Die where it feels like Craig and the director are taking this all a little bit too seriously. No Time to Die is constantly groping for a subtext and meaning which doesn't always exist.

After five films there is nowhere left to take Daniel Craig's version of Bond. A pang of deja vu therefore hovers over proceedings with the recycled retired Bond angle and the continued presence of Madeleine. In a sense one can understand why Craig and EON liked the idea of killing Bond off at the end of this film. If nothing else it pulled the rug out from under the viewer in a way that these final flickering embers of the Craig era probably wouldn't otherwise have done.

We do of course have the death of Felix Leiter too in No Time to Die but this obviously has less weight given that Felix is a background character and wasn't even in the last two films anyway. Poor old Felix. he doesn't have much luck in either 007 continuity. Attacked by sharks and shot! Billy Magnussen plays Leiter's CIA colleague Logan Ash - who turns out to be a double agent working for Safin. Ash shoots Leiter on a boat - which leads to waterlogged death for Felix and affords Daniel Craig another chance to be anguished and sad (Daniel Craig is never an actor to pass up an opportunity to look anguished and sad). It is unavoidably depressing to see Felix Leiter kick the bucket but, look on the bright side, at some point he'll doubtless be back right as rain in future films played by a different actor!

Sadly, Lashana Lynch's Nomi doesn't threaten to justify all the marketing hype that this character enjoyed during the many promotional campaigns for No Time to Die. There isn't much spark or chemistry at all between Craig and Lynch and after her early introduction (where she warns Bond to kept his nose of MI6's affairs and then has some action capers in the Cuba sequence) it feels like Nomi never really has quite enough to do. She's on the fringes of the film until the last act - when she gets to go on a mission with Bond. Nomi is actually quite arrogant and annoying at first but does soften somewhat later and hand the 007 codename back to Bond. You could actually describe this as a bit sexist if you were so inclined! Gratuitous trivia - Bond's code number '007' was apparently inspired by a bus route in Kent which was often taken by the author Ian Fleming.

The hysterical coverage about a (largely mythical) backlash concerning Lynch's casting made it seem like Lashana was playing Bond in this film. Nomi is simply 007 now that Bond has retired. Even in the third act (which should have been her chance to really shine) Nomi comes across as a generic action character. She is even made to look like a spare wheel in some of the MI6 scenes. Nomi is likeable enough in the end but you can't help feeling that they never quite managed to flesh this character out sufficiently to give Lashana Lynch a real chance to show her charisma. The verbal sparring between Bond and Nomi also lacks wit - which is obviously the fault of the writers and not the actors. If you took Nomi out of this film it wouldn't really make much difference at all or weaken it in any way. After the ink afforded to the character in the promotion of No Time to Die you can only describe this as disappointing.

There isn't too much evidence of the famed wit of Phoebe Waller-Bridge in No Time to Die's script (in fact, what puns we do get are pretty bad) but Waller-Bridge can be praised for the Cuba scenes involving Ana de Armas as Paloma. Paloma's character and scenes were apparently a late addition crafted by Waller-Bridge and Paloma all but steals the film.

Ana de Armas is amusing and charismatic and more than makes the most of her brief contribution to No Time to Die - to the point where we are rather sad to see her go so soon. Ana de Armas and Daniel Craig, who worked together on the murder mystery film Knives Out, have a nice easygoing light-hearted chemistry which is palpably absent when Craig shares the screen with the other female characters in this movie. Craig's otherwise grumpy and tightly wound Bond seems at his most relaxed and natural in these Cuba scenes.

One suspects that what makes the Paloma scenes enjoyable is the fact that they serve as light relief in what is often quite a grim film (for a Bond movie). What is interesting about the Paloma and Bond scenes is that their relationship is purely professional (as Timothy Dalton's Bond might say) and Paloma quickly quashes any suggestion of a sexual or romantic connection. In fact, Paloma literally recoils at the mere notion of anything happening between them. Never before has the Bond series so explicitly had Bond rejected by a woman because he's too old! You couldn't imagine this happening in the Roger Moore films. There is of course a slight contradiction in this approach though because Ana de Armas is only a few years younger than Léa Seydoux in real life. Maybe they were working on the assumption that Seydoux's character seems and looks more mature that Paloma?

Phoebe Waller-Bridge makes Paloma independent and sort of quirky and the character (thanks in no small part to the talent of the actor who plays her) is immediately likeable and charismatic. This is aided by the fact that Paloma is wearing the same dress Barbara Bach had on at the pyramids in The Spy Who Loved Me (No Time to Die, as we have noted, is awash with these little references to previous Bond films). The fact that Bond and Palma have no love scene is doubtless in part because Paloma isn't in the film for very long but the twenty year age gap between Craig and Ana de Armas appears to be a factor - which, as we have noted, is novel for Bond. Roger Moore and Pierce Brosnan's Bonds would have had no qualms or trouble at all seducing someone young enough to be their daughter. One could cite this element as the script reflecting Bond's age and also being more sensitive to the prevailing times. The Bond in No Time to Die is not the habitual womaniser of the past.

You can't help wondering if No Time to Die might have been more purely enjoyable if Paloma had enjoyed a much more extended role in the plot but then it's difficult to see how there would have been enough room for this character without major changes to the script. It's hard to see specifically how there could have been room for Nomi and Paloma as both are agents and similarish sorts of characters in that sense. The roles afforded to both Madeleine and Nomi would probably have had to be drastically cut or jettisoned to make room for Paloma. It would be nice to think that perhaps Ana de Armas could return to the Bond franchise one day and play a different character. They did this with Maud Adams so why not? Paloma is fun and could have been a classic Bond Girl had she featured as the lead in a more conventional sort of Bond film.

The sets for the Cuban scenes (this is a very romantic Hollywood depiction of Cuba - which is fair enough because this is a Bond movie) are quite superb. In fact, the production design as a whole on No Time to Die is, as one might expect, of the highest quality. The action sequence where Paloma and bond gatecrash a Spectre party is the film at its most generic (you could easily imagine this sequence in a Brosnan Bond film) but it is enjoyable and offers standard 007 fun of the type that No Time to Die often decides to eschew in favour of drama and exposition. The spark provided by Ana de Armas is certainly missed in No Time to Die once her (sadly all too brief) participation is over. Farewell Paloma. We hardly knew you.

When the film moves back to London there isn't that much for Ben Whishaw as Q or Naomie Harris as Moneypenny to do - although Ralph Fiennes as M, by contrast, does have a bit more meat to his part than usual. M seems to be in an especially bad mood in this film (which is understandable given the circumstances of the plot) and his scenes with Bond are unusually fractious and even bitter at times. You rather get the impression that Ralph Fiennes asked for a bit more drama and tension to sink his teeth into when it came to M and the script certainly caters to this desire. I did not enjoy the fact that M swears in this film though. Bond films have always traditionally been for all ages (most of us got into Bond films watching them on television as kids) and family entertainment so one would hope that the franchise doesn't make a habit of dropping stray cuss words in the films going forward. It just feels a bit awkward and jarring to have a character in Bond drop in the F-word.

It is established in this film that Q is gay. Bond and Moneypenny turn up at his house at one point because they require his technological sleuthing. Q is preparing dinner for a gentlemen he is expecting to arrive. This scene provides a bit more lightness to the movie and is pleasant enough. Whishaw did grumble later though about the fact that we never got to see Q's boyfriend in person. It doesn't really matter either way. It is around this point of No Time to Die that the film's unusual length (for a Bond movie) begins to become apparent and something of a problem. There is no reason why any Bond film should be nearly three hours long. This isn't Lord of the Rings or Gone with the Wind. No Time to Die doesn't have enough memorable action set-pieces and fun to completely sustain our attention over such a long running time and so the exposition and Bond/Madeleine melodrama inevitably begins to outstay its welcome in the end.

We now have an interminable scene between Swann and Safin. Safin's mumbling dialogue is hard to pick up at the best of times. Indeed, the sound mixing on No Time to Die is quite poor overall with dialogue drowned out by music and sound FX and some lines difficult to pick up because everyone insists on whispering or mumbling their dialogue. Actors talking softly or whispering seems to be a strange modern trend in film and television. In 2017, the BBC aired a history miniseries called SS-GB (which took place in an alternative timeline where the Nazis successfully invaded Britain and featured former fringe Bond contender Sam Riley) and were deluged with complaints from viewers because they couldn't hear a word that the mumbling sotto voce actors were saying!

Safin infects Madeleine with the nanobot virus because he wants to use her to USE Bond to unwittingly kill Blofeld. Christoph Waltz's brief return as Blofeld is disappointing to say the least and both Waltz and Daniel Craig appear to have saved one of their bad acting days for this bizarre scene. Waltz doesn't even appear to be taking his participation in No Time to Die here very seriously. His brief cameo in the film is camp and eccentric. Michael G. Wilson's promise that Blofeld would be bigger and badder than ever in No Time to Die turns out to be a case of false advertising. In fact, Blofeld is hardly in the film at all. One would have to say that EON clearly had no idea what to do with Blofeld after his return to the franchise for Spectre and No Time to Die. Let us hope that they do something more memorable with the character should he return again in the future.

Daniel Craig, by contrast, egregiously over eggs this Blofeld scene and seems to be taking it TOO seriously. Had Martin Campbell been directing this scene, his glasses perched on his nose with a piece of string like Larry Grayson, I like to imagine he would have gently asked Daniel Craig to tone it down a few notches and then simply done another take.

Leiter and Blofeld have now bitten the dust in this movie. The era of Daniel Craig is going for a scorched earth policy as it slowly draws to a close. The lights are going off one by one. All the bridges are being blown up with dynamite. Nothing is being left behind!

No Time to Die now throws the focus back on Bond and Madeleine as they reconcile and Bond learns that she has a daughter named Mathilde. It will of course transpire that Mathilde is Bond's daughter. The rumours concerning this twist were therefore true. This twist was decidedly not what you could call everyone's cup of tea when it comes to Bond fans. It plunged the Craig era even further into the dramatic soap opera-rish elements that EON seemed determined to shoehorn into the franchise. Only two children have ever had a speaking role in a Bond film. This happened in Diamonds Are Forever and The Man with the Golden Gun. Child actors and Bond films do not traditionally mix.

The main problem with giving Bond a child and then placing this child in peril for the purposes of tension that that we've already seen this plot in a billion movies from Commando to Taken. It is just about the least original movie plot device imaginable! If I had tuppence for each time I'd watched an action or horror movie where a child is placed in peril then I'd be a very rich man. In the novels by Ian Fleming, Bond had a child with Kissy Suzuki ** but he is unaware that she is pregnant and the child doesn't feature again (unless you count Raymond Benson's short story Blast from the Past - which most people probably don't). I'd imagine some Bond fans could have happily lived without Bond having a child in No Time to Die but then this is Craig's last hurrah and all bets are off. Just about every idea that EON and Craig have ever had concerning Bond films - however left-field or unconventional - is seen as a viable ingredient in No Time to Die.

One can't help having some sympathy with Charlie Higson, the author of the Young Bond novels. In 2022, Higson said of No Time to Die - "Bond is a fantasy, he's got no wife, no kids, you rarely see him at home, he lives in hotels, eats in restaurants, sleeps with as many women as he wants and gets to kill people. You don't have to worry about a back story or any boring discussions with his girlfriend. Which is why I absolutely hate No Time To Die. They put in all the boring stuff you don't want. The start of the film is great – he's in a really flash car, having a car chase around Matera. But he's got his girlfriend with him and they're having a row. What kind of fantasy is that? Find the ejector seat button, get rid of her and have an adventure."

The big chase chase sequence in a Norwegian forest (which, as we noted in my previous No Time to Die book was actually shot in Scotland) feels rather flat in terms of its action and features some less than perfect CGI. No Time to Die features more CGI than any other Bond film but thankfully this CGI is not of the Die Another Day iceberg para-surfing variety but simply, for the most part, embellishments to backdrop scenery. It is only really during sections of this first chase that the FX standards seemed to slip a few notches with the flying cars. Bond gains revenge on Ash in this sequence in what seems to be a little homage to the way Roger Moore dispatched Michael Gothard in For Your Eyes Only.

One notable thing about the forest chase which does work though is that it takes place in a thick foggy mist. Like the pre-credit sequence, this feels like Fukunaga enjoyably throwing in another horror themed inspiration. Live and Let Die is the only Bond film previously that overtly leans into the horror genre. No Time to Die does have plenty of atmosphere in some of these more diverting flourishes by Fukunaga. On the evidence of No Time to Die you wouldn't say that Fukunaga is the most exciting director when it comes to action but in terms of style he does make the film look consistently stylish and interesting.

Nomi is now thrust back into the spotlight and must infiltrate Safin's headquarters in a glider with Bond. We are now temporarily lurched into a Roger Moore film or Die Another Day - which is fine because No Time to Die was becoming somewhat gloomy and draggy anyway. We move steadily towards the inevitable showdown between Bond and Safin. This encounter is not terribly helped by the fact that we are still more than a trifle foggy on who Safin is and what he exactly he wants. He simply appears to be an anarchist. He's just mad. Daniel Craig and Rami Malek do their level best to bring some meaning and dramatic heft to this encounter but it feels too little too late.

The last act feels dragged out but there are some good fight scenes and action set-pieces to mitigate this. Nomi manages to get Swann and Mathilde to safety but Bond, who had eventually shot Safin, has to stay to open the silo doors so that the Royal Navy can destroy the biological threat with missiles. Bond has been infected with the virus and so decides that he must sacrifice himself to do this one last thing. Bond knows that he can never be with his family again in the true sense because he is deadly to the touch. He has a sentimental last chat with Madeleine before he is blown to atoms by missiles. The film piles on the treacle and overblown music for this unexpected death scene.

M and the staff at MI6 drink a toast to the late James Bond (this must surely rank as one of the most depressing scenes in the history of the franchise - but then maybe that was the intention?) and go back to their desks. No Time to Die then ends with Mathilde and Madeleine driving off as Madeleine says she'll tell her daughter about a man named James Bond. The love theme from OHMSS gratingly kicks in (again) over the credits.

So, they actually killed off James Bond? Was this necessary? Does it matter? Well, to answer the last question, no, it probably doesn't matter. James Bond (as the end credits promise) will return and No Time to Die will fade into the past. The next Bond will not be the same version of Bond as Craig's Bond. Those days when Bond actors were all essentially playing the same person (references to Bond's doomed OHMSS marriage were present in the Moore and Dalton eras) well and truly ended with Craig's Bond. Craig's Bond never even met Tracey let alone married her. The Craig incarnation of the character was its own thing and distinct from what came before (and after). As such, EON obviously felt they had a licence to do whatever they wanted in his last movie. They had a licence to kill Bond!

No Time to Die is awash with themes which have been persistent in most of the Craig era. An obsession with conspiracies and shadowy people who pull the strings in the world. The most recurring theme in the Craig era by this fifth film is an ongoing obsession with Bond's relevance in the world. In a world of bioweapons, enemies who hide in the shadows, and high tech surveillance, is there any need for 007? The problem with this theme is that the scripts are taking James Bond too seriously. James Bond has nothing in common with real spies in the real world. Spies do not drive gadget laden Aston Martins and travel around the world killing people! James Bond is a fun movie fantasy character. You can make the films more grounded and tougher but to dig too deeply into Bond as a character and obsess over the nature of his profession and his relevance in an (as Paul McCartney might sing) ever-changing world simply becomes tiresome and pretentious navel-gazing in the end.

It isn't as if this theme is new to Bond. It featured in

GoldenEye when M called Bond a Cold War relic. The script for GoldenEye did touch upon the notion of Bond as an anachronism in a new world. It didn't hammer this theme to death though. It isn't as if Pierce Brosnan's Bond spent that film moping around and questioning if he wanted to be a secret agent anymore. GoldenEye was the first Bond film produced since the collapse of the Soviet Union and the end of the Cold War. In the long (legal induced) hiatus after Licence to Kill there was some understandable degree of debate about the relevance of Bond movies anymore and speculation about how they would have to change in order to have any future as we neared the 21st Century. GoldenEye's script addresses these concerns by having a new female M and paying lightish lip-service to the fact that the Cold War has ended and so it is now more difficult to actually deduce who the enemies are supposed to be.

The threat still comes from Russia in GoldenEye but it is engineered by a British former spy who was once friends with Bond. GoldenEye acknowledges that the world is now a murkier and more complex place and also offers a meta commentary on doubts about the relevance of the franchise. This is all very secondary though to the traditional bells and whistles of a Bond film. GoldenEye is not an especially grounded or gritty Bond film. It has some enjoyably daft action sequences and plenty of humour. GoldenEye has a few 'relevance' themes but these themes are not used for melodrama or angst. They do not dominate the story. The more you mine into Bond's relevance and history the more shallow it becomes. Bond is essentially a tabula rasa. If you dig too deep there isn't much there and this leads to screenwriters having to make stupid stuff up - like the Blofeld step-brother angle.

My own personal preference is for the Timothy Dalton era approach. Dalton, like Craig, presented a more down to earth and straight laced interpretation of Bond. However, the two Dalton films were fairly traditional adventures (I suppose you could argue that Licence to Kill was slightly atypical with its violence) and do not endlessly question Bond's relevance in the world or constantly dredge up his backstory. In No Time to Die, Bond is given these big dramatic speeches when he encounters Blofeld and Safin and Craig delivers them like he's doing Hamlet. The problem is though that we often have no idea what Bond is even talking about or why his knickers are in such an almighty twist in the first place. The drama feels hollow and vague.

Now, as you may have detected in this chapter, I am not the biggest fan of No Time to Die. The main problem for me is that I was never emotionally invested in the relationship between Bond and Madeleine and so the drama and emotion of this film fell completely flat. Ultimately, I just didn't care about Madeleine Swann and so for me personally this film had a very shaky dramatic foundation. The concept of the cinematic Bond having a child is one I dislike and so this was another obstacle in my path when it came to enjoying this film. No Time to Die is a film of bold narrative decisions and you'll either like those choices or feel like you could have happily lived without them.

Bond's death felt overwrought and unnecessary to me. I would include myself with those Bond fans who feel that Spectre (which I think is a trifle underrated when it comes to the Craig era pictures) would have been a better swansong for Daniel Craig and that we should have just left his 007 to drive off into the sunset in his Aston Martin. No Time to Die feels like a film that is trying too hard. It feels too long and overstuffed and Daniel Craig and the director seem like they are taking it all a tad too seriously. No Time to Die has an inflated sense of its own importance.

This is merely my own opinion though and if you think No Time to Die was fantastic that's perfectly fine and equally as valid too. Many Bond fans DID love No Time to Die and would strongly disagree with my own thoughts on the movie. In fact, some Bond fans think No Time to Die is a masterpiece. We all have different opinions on the films and that's part of the fun of being a Bond fan. For example, I love the two Timothy

Dalton films but am aware they leave some fans cold. For all its goofiness, I actually love Moonraker too but understand why some fans would find it too silly and cartoonish. It would be dull indeed if Bond fans agreed on everything. It just goes to show that, with Bond fans at least, you can't please everyone all the time.

No Time to Die was definitely what you might describe as a strong cheese in the canon. Some loved it, some thought it was middling, and others hated it. While some of us would have been happy to jettison the backstory and melodrama and just have a zippy escapist adventure this was never likely to happen. EON were determined that Craig's last film would be an 'event' and take a few risks. Whether or not the end result justified this artistic gamble is all in the eye of the beholder. It should probably be stressed though that critics and general audiences, in the majority, seemed to like No Time to Die. It was specifically Bond fans (like me) who had the most polarised reaction. In a way though this was all good. So long as Bond fans are still arguing over James Bond then the series is alive, provoking debate, vibrant, and even healthy. Doubtless the next film in the series, which is liable to be completely different from No Time to Die, will also provoke plenty of fan debate too!

* The grand tradition of the PTS (pre-title sequence) featuring a spectacular stunt involving James Bond was only really established in 1977's The Spy Who Loved Me when Bond memorably skied off a mountain ledge in a banana yellow ski-suit to evade various gun toting goons. After that it was expected (and hugely anticipated) that each Bond film would begin with a jawdropping stunt sequence. Before the tradition established by The Spy Who loved Me, the pre-title sequences were a little more experimental and unpredictable. Sure, sometimes you got Bond involved in stunts and action (like Goldfinger and Thunderball) but they also had more licence to do something slightly strange or moody.

From Russia with Love marks the introduction of many

elements and people that would become staples of the series, like the pre-title sequence and title credits with dancing girls - or in this case a bellydancer. The pre-title sequence in From Russia with Love is rather atmospheric and features Bond apparently being hunted around a moonlit mansion at night by Red Grant. It's all a SPECTRE training exercise though and this ersatz Bond comes to a very nasty end. The first pre-title sequences in the Roger Moore films are notable for the fact that they (aside from a waxwork dummy - which is patently Roger Moore standing still) don't feature Bond at all.

George Lazenby breaks the fourth wall at the end of the PTS of On Her Majesty's Secret Service by saying - "This never happened to the other fella!" This was a line Lazenby said on the set all the time so the director Peter Hunt decided to have him say it in the film. Harry Saltzman was the person who came up with the idea of having a pre-credit sequence in the Bond films. The PTS of Octopussy has Bond taking control of a miniature Acrostar jet in an unnamed Central American country and dodging a heat-seeking missile before destroying an aircraft hanger in spectacular fashion. Nothing was too stupid or expensive to put in a James Bond film in those days and that was essentially the charm of the series.

** You Only Live Twice is the 12th of thirteen James Bond novels written by Ian Fleming and the last to be published (in 1964) while he was alive. This book was an influence on the depiction of Safin in No Time to Die. The novel follows on from the shocking events of On Her Majesty's Secret Service - a book you should probably read before you pick up this one. In You Only Live Twice, James Bond is a broken man and M decides that the only thing to do is to send him on an apparently impossible mission to either waken his senses or end his career. Bond is asked to secure access to Magic 44, a Japanese project that reveals the transmissions of secret Soviet radio broadcasts.

After tracking down Tiger Tanaka, head of Japan's version of SIS, Bond discovers the Japanese already have Blue Route, a secret Chinese system which Bond had hoped to trade for Magic 44. Bond is shown some elements of Magic 44 which are vitally important to British security and offered more access if he undertakes a mission for Tanaka and the Japanese. A mysterious and dangerous 'Swiss botanist' known as Dr Shatterhand has opened a deadly 'garden of death' in an old Japanese castle stocked with poisonous specimens of plants and animals. 007 must visit this lethal location and kill Dr Shatterhand.

One of Fleming's most famous Bond novels, You Only Live Twice sees the author experiment with a more character driven piece that contains a surreal and vivid atmosphere. The focus here is on Bond himself who is gradually falling to pieces after the events of On Her Majesty's Secret Service and faces one of his most macabre missions. The plot is perhaps rather contrived with Bond asked to investigate Shatterhand, who just happens to be a very famous old adversary, but it does set up an epic final battle of wills that reminds one of the Sherlock Holmes/Moriaty relationship. The destiny of these men is somehow always going to be linked. You Only Live Twice is very travelogue at times and you are immersed in Japanese culture right from the beginning of the book. Fleming's descriptions of architecture, ninjutsu, food ("James Bond wrestled with his chopsticks and slivers of raw octopus and a mound of rice") and simple Japanese village life are certainly descriptive, giving the book a rich exotic atmosphere. As ever with Fleming, parts of the novel and certain attitudes are rather dated though. The depiction of Japan, for example, sometimes leans towards it being a fairly primitive place.

Fleming, as usual, weaves a large degree of factual information and passages about Japanese culture into his story, which does help ingrain the reader in the location of the novel. This habit can sometimes be slightly intrusive and 'tacked-on', but it works reasonably well here. "Technically, this would be a geisha of low caste," writes Fleming. "She would not be proficient in the traditional arts of her calling -- she would not be able to tell humorous stories, sing, paint, or compose verses about her patron. But, unlike her cultured sisters, she might agree to perform more robust services -- discreetly, of course, in conditions of the utmost privacy and at a high price. But to the boorish, brutalized tastes of a gaijin, a foreigner, this made more sense than having a tanka of thirty-one syllables, which in any case he couldn't understand, equate in exquisite language, his charms with budding chrysanthemums on the slopes of Mount Fuji."

Strengths of the book include Bond's sometimes touching relationship with Kissy Suzuki and the many sections where Bond lives a simple life in a serene Japanese village, disguised as 'coalminer' Taro Todoroki as he trains and prepares for his visit to Dr Shatterhand's deadly garden. It's a bit daft the notion that Bond could realistically turn himself into a convincing Japanese but then this is a James Bond adventure. To be fair to Fleming, Bond's disguise proves far from impenetrable and it was a lot less convincing in the film version where a 6'3 Sean Connery attempted to pass himself off as a simple Japanese villager!

The beautiful Kissy, who was a Hollywood star before choosing a life as a fisherwoman, is a strong Bond girl who comes across as independent and free of the anguished past and neurotic inclinations of some of Fleming's other female heroines. There are some nice passages where Bond and Kissy dive for sea shells and, amusingly, Kissy reveals that the only man who was truly kind to her was the actor David Niven, who, as all Bond anoraks will know, was one of Fleming's suggestions to play Bond when the film series began in 1962. Although Fleming was not immune from contradicting himself from time to time (Bond hates beef here but lives on it in other books), part of the fun of these books is information about Bond himself that is included within the story. We learn here, amongst other things, that Bond is currently still under forty, weighs 183 pounds, and has bungled two missions between this book and On Her Majesty's Secret Service, leading M to suspect the ailing agent might be a security risk.

Unlike the film version, one of the most fantastical and money strewn of the series, there are few large set-pieces in Fleming's You Only Live Twice, which unfolds relatively slowly. The book is certainly engrossing at times though with Shatterhand's haunting 'garden of death', a weird device and location that the reader becomes very curious to know more about. The book benefits from strong characters like Bond's Australian contact Dikko Henderson and Tiger Tanaka, the head of the Japanese Secret Service. Bond's interactions with them are very entertaining in places and the relationships are nicely conveyed. "For the time being," says Tiger on Japan's relationship with the United States. "We are being subjected to what I can best describe as the Scuola di Coca-Cola. Baseball, amusement arcades, hot dogs, hideously large bosoms, neon lighting - these are part of our payment for defeat in battle."

The book moves towards a truly dark climax in the castle featuring the 'Question Room', a swordfight and further shocking developments regarding Bond himself. You Only Live Twice has a real air of madness and melancholia at times. It's an introspective book in the series that makes up for the lack of sweep and action with a macabre air and excellent characters. You Only Live Twice is an interesting entry in Fleming's series, best read in conjunction with On Her Majesty's Secret Service. It isn't perfect by any means and some readers might find it a tad slow at times, but it's a richly atmospheric book with some decidedly strange elements and some big twists and turns in the never dull life of James Bond.

The popular children's author Roald Dahl wrote the movie version of You Only Live Twice. Dahl met Ian Fleming during the war and the pair had been friends. Not much of the novel was retained in the film treatment. "You Only Live Twice was the only Fleming book that had virtually no semblance of a plot that could be made into a movie," said Dahl. "The concept of Blofeld patrolling his garden of poisonous plants in a medieval suit of armour and lopping off the heads of half-blinded Japanese was ridiculous. When I began the script, I could retain only four or five of the original novel's story ideas.

Obviously, the movie had to take place in Japan. We kept Blofeld and Tiger Tanaka and Bond's pearl-diving girlfriend, Kissy Suzuki. And we retained the Ninjas – those masters of oriental martial arts who use their talents to raid Blofeld's hideout. But aside from those bits, I had nothing except a wonderful Ian Fleming title."

# CHAPTER FIVE - AFTERMATH

Cary Fukunaga was interviewed for Slashfilm in October and said that although some sets were actually designed and constructed for Danny Boyle's aborted Bond film they didn't use any of them in No Time to Die - although they did briefly consider it. Given that Boyle's film had a Russian theme it would appear likely that most of the sets were simply irrelevant to what No Time to Die eventually became. No Time to Die obviously didn't have much use for a Russian gulag! Fukunaga said that when he had met with Barbara Broccoli prior to Danny Boyle being signed on as the director, he'd pitched an idea for a Bond reboot film. None of the ideas in this reboot pitch were used in No Time to Die so Fukunaga felt his pitch (which he obviously kept to himself) would still be viable for the next Bond film. Cary Fukunaga was asked about whether or not he would like to direct another Bond film in the future and said he was certainly open to that possibility. He would be happy to take the phone call should EON contact him again.

Fukunaga said that the ending of No Time to Die had been something that Barbara Broccoli and Daniel Craig both insisted upon. Fukunaga said it was difficult to come up with a way to do this (kill Bond) but he felt that in the end they managed to connect Bond's sacrifice in No Time to Die to themes already prevalent in the Daniel Craig era. Cary Fukunaga was somewhat vague on what exactly these themes were were but seemed to suggest it had something to do with characters being doomed by their professions. Fukunaga said they had considered blowing Bond up in a rocket and having him shot by an unknown bullet before they decided on missiles as the best way to kill him. Daniel Craig joked that they should have had Bond killed by a dodgy oyster!

It was reported in the media at this time that MGM had $1 million a month interest charges on the money it had borrowed to finance No Time to Die. This had affected the studio's financial credit rating on the markets. The film had cost a whopping $250 million to produce. When you factor in the many millions spent in all the marketing campaigns it amounted to an eye-watering total. No wonder MGM were so desperate in 2021 to get the film out so that they could finally start making some of that money back. Money was clearly going to be less of a problem going forward for an Amazon owned MGM. Amazon were perfectly happy and able to spend hundreds of millions on streaming television shows let alone movies. If nothing else, Amazon had deep pockets. Money would not be an issue on Bond 26.

Despite the preposterously delayed and complex release history of No Time to Die, it was hardly unique. Top Gun: Maverick was actually postponed SIX times during the pandemic.

MGM decided to move No Time to Die onto PVOD platforms one month after it was released in cinemas. This was a shrewd tactic because it did very well and managed to catch some of those Bond fans and casual fans who were still reluctant to go out in throngs of crowds to public places. This move was something of a compromise between MGM and EON. This way, Barbara Broccoli still got her swanky premiere and cinema release but MGM also got some extra VOD money.

The film also got a limited re-release in cinemas later on - which added a few extra pennies to the gross. As of yet, the deal for Amazon to purchase MGM had not gone through. That would be completed in March 2022. Spare a thought by the way for Australian Bond fans at this time. No Time to Die didn't open there until November the 11th. Heaven knows how they avoided any spoilers. In the end, No Time to Die would gross around £770 million at the worldwide box-office. This was a very respectable figure under the circumstances (No Time to Die was the first film since the COVID-19 pandemic that crossed $100 million in an overseas debut without the China market) but down on Spectre and even further down on Skyfall. The fact that it didn't make as much money as those films was completely expected and probably unavoidable.

Trade publications suggested that MGM would take a financial hit on No Time to Die because it needed to gross at least $900 million to show any real profit. At the very least though EON knew that interest in James Bond was still very high and they were doubtless comforted by the fact that the next film was highly unlikely to experience such a protracted and frustrating series of delays. Most importantly of all, the next Bond film would hopefully only require ONE promotional campaign! MGM and product placement partners had spent hundreds of millions of dollars promoting No Time to Die across its various aborted campaigns and release dates. EON would be desperately hoping that such a pesky and expensive scenario never happened again.

Interestingly, one article on the finances and box-office of No Time to Die said that with the modern Bond films EON increasingly made Britain a priority in their marketing and release dates because of the huge amounts of money the films made there. The strategy of EON was therefore to maximise the huge demand for Bond in Britain and allow this to mitigate the fact that North America is not always quite such a sure thing (in terms of blockbuster status) when it comes to 007. Another mitigating factor was that Bond films could also now rely on making a very welcome bundle of cash in China. Bond was a very global brand - so little wonder that Amazon wanted a slice of this indestructible pop culture icon. When tallied together, the box-office revenue collected by No Time to Die in Britain and China eclipsed that of the United States.

Neal Purvis and Robert Wade were interviewed in The

Guardian at this time and were likeably self-deprecating and modest discussing their up and down contribution to Bond. The duo said that they had worked on the script for what eventually became No Time to Die in 2017 and had it had been read and agreed by Daniel Craig. Then Danny Boyle came along and threw their script out because he wanted John Hodge to write a new story for him. After the departure of Boyle, Purvis & Wade dug their script back out and it became the basis for No Time to Die. The DNA weapon McGuffin in No Time to Die was a very old idea because it had first been floated for use in the 1999 film The World is Not Enough.

Purvis and Wade said that they had tried to prod at the formula in Bond films so that a few more unexpected things could happen. In an interesting titbit, they seemed to suggest that Pierce Brosnan had been irritated by Judi Dench's M being the main focal point for the villain in The World is Not Enough. Purvis and Wade downplayed the suggestion that gender politics and political correctness was now a huge factor in Bond scripts. They said they just try to write a good Bond script and don't obsess over such matters.

The duo said they had no idea if they would be back to write the next Bond film. Those decisions had yet to be made. They did believe though that James Bond would always be around in the future and that was still plenty of life left in the franchise. You certainly wouldn't have bet against Purvis and Wade writing again on Bond films in the future because Barbara Broccoli clearly has a high opinion of them. One amusing detail in the Guardian interview was that Purvis and Wade said they often listened to the Jason Bourne soundtrack to get in the mood when they wrote Bond movies!

In November, it was revealed that Daniel Craig had asked for his incarnation of Bond to be killed off in his final film way back in 2005 when he first took the role. This torpedoed the speculation that Danny Boyle had left the movie because he'd wanted to kill Bond off but EON didn't. EON were clearly perfectly happy to bump Craig's Bond off at the end of his last bow. Boyle seemed to suggest, when asked about No Time to Die, that he had no problems with Bond being killed off in the film. John Hodge, in an interview with The Guardian, said that Barbara Broccoli and Daniel Craig had explicitly asked for Bond to have a death scene so this was always something that HAD to be included. Hodge said he always got the impression that what EON really wanted to get rid of him and keep Danny Boyle. In the end though Boyle's loyalty to Hodge made him walk away too.

Hodge said that only a line of his dialogue made it into No Time to Die in the end. I'd imagine Bond fans would love to read John Hodge's script. Hodge seemed to give the impression in his Guardian interview that writing a big action film like Bond hadn't really been his cup of tea and that he was relieved to have left in the end. John Hodge said the most difficult thing about writing a Bond film is coming up with original action sequences that haven't been done before either in the Bond franchise or other action adventures. It is almost impossible now to come up with something that hasn't already been done elsewhere.

Daniel Craig said that after the German premiere of Casino Royale, he had asked Barbara Broccoli how many Bond films he was expected to make and she replied that they had him under contract for four films. Craig then asked if his Bond could die onscreen when he got to his last film. Barbara apparently laughed this off but did agree to a death scene. This conversation was then forgotten but after he agreed to come back after Spectre, Craig remembered the chat about a death scene for his Bond and resurrected this idea. Barbara Broccoli was more than happy to go along with this. A big factor in EON'S obvious enthusiasm for this idea was most likely the huge success of the James Mangold film Logan - where Wolverine was given a heroic death to mark the end of Hugh Jackman's tenure as this character.

"I feel like I needed to end what I did on it," said Craig on Bond's death. "I would be only satisfied if I could walk away and there was nowhere else for that to go, that someone else would have to come along and invent something completely different. If he stayed alive he would kill the people he loved, so, therefore there was no argument."

It was pretty remarkable to think that a Bond actor could exert this level of artistic control over the franchise. Craig was very unique in that regard. The previous Bond actors basically had to turn up to work and then play what was given to them. Craig on the other was given a lot of power in deciding WHAT he was going to turn up to play.

"It's the ultimate sacrifice," said Barbara Broccoli on Bond's demise in No Time to Die. "It's very appropriate because people in this line of work put themselves at risk all the time. The amazing thing was that the audience managed to keep this secret, and that's really a testament, I think, to the Bond fans, that they didn't want to spoil other people's enjoyment by telling them the end of the story." Barbara said that she felt the death of Bond in No Time to Die was a great way to put a line under the Craig era so that they could then begin afresh with a completely clean slate the next time around.

Léa Seydoux and Naomie Harris both said they were shocked when they first read the No Time to Die script and saw that Bond dies at the end. Harris said that she therefore felt a great responsibility when it came to secrecy. The cast were obviously required not to discuss any twists before the film came out. Bond fans themselves seemed to be quite sharply divided on Bond's death No Time to Die. It was a bit of a sore point for many and triggered some lively forum debates. No Time to Die appears to be the Marmite Bond film when it comes to the Bond fan community. You either love it or hate it. Some Bond fans felt No time to Die was a masterpiece and worth the wait. Others wish it hadn't been made at all. A forum bun fight greeted its arrival.

'It's The Last Jedi of Bond movies,' complained one MI6 forum member. 'Subversive, melodramatic garbage that went out of it's way to make pretty much all the core characters look bad or just tear them down wholesale. It was also pretty boring after the first hour. It was a bloated mess of a film. Very much style over substance. If I wanted to watch a soap opera I'd tune into it on the tv.' On the other hand, there were other forum views like this - 'Personally, I thought it was the complete opposite of style over substance/shock value. I thought the ending matched up really well with the themes they'd been exploring throughout this era. Bond ruining everything he touches, lost childhoods leading to screwed up people. Bond realising he was too far gone to have a normal life, and sacrificing himself to ensure his daughter could, was the most heroic I've found the character since Dalton took down Sanchez. Loved it, and while I would have been happy with Spectre as an ending at the time, I'm really glad Craig decided to return with hindsight.'

Articles at this time were full of theories about how Bond might be resurrected in the next film after his shock demise in No Time to Die. What these articles failed to understand was that it didn't actually matter. The next film would simply ignore the Craig continuity and forget No Time to Die! There were though some fans who suggested that Craig could actually be brought back in a sort of loose adaptation of Fleming's The Man with the Golden Gun. The Man with the Golden Gun is the thirteenth James Bond novel written by Ian Fleming and was first published, posthumously, in 1965. The book begins with Bond - who was missing presumed dead because of the events of You Only Live Twice where he ended the story suffering from amnesia after an epic final encounter with Blofeld - turning up in London again and being granted an audience with M.

However, during the meeting, Bond begins to rabidly extol the benefits and superiority of communism and then attempts to murder M with a stream of liquid cyanide. He is foiled and apprehended and it transpires that 007 had been brainwashed by the Russians in Vladivostok - a place he had gone to seeking to unlock something about his past. Bond is duly deprogrammed and restored to something resembling his old self by electroshock therapy. Retirement seems the most likely option for our troubled hero but M decides instead to give Bond a new - and quite possibly last - mission. Bond is asked to travel to the Caribbean to terminate Francisco "Pistols" Scaramanga, a legendary killer known as "The Man with the Golden Gun" for his chosen instrument of choice, a gold-plated Colt 45. The feared Scaramanga is backed by Cuba and is known to be responsible for the deaths of several British agents. If Bond succeeds he can perhaps be of use to Queen and Country again, if he fails he will become Scaramanga's latest and most famous victim.

Well, you could probably, at a push imagine a Bond film where Craig's Bond is still somehow alive after the events of No Time to Die but suffering from amnesia or something. It was all purely academic anyway. Daniel Craig was liable to be pushing 60 by the time the next Bond film came out. He was definitely finished with the franchise and more than happy to move on with his life and career. As much as Barbara Broccoli might desire this, you couldn't keep wheeling Daniel Craig back until he was an old age pensioner! The franchise was at one of those tricky but necessary crossroads points where it needed to relaunch itself with a fresh coat of paint and a younger actor.

The longevity of the Bond franchise was in large part down to the fact that it periodically reinvented itself and changed the lead actor. In this it was rather like Doctor Who. If you don't like an incarnation of Doctor Who or think it has gone stale you can take comfort in the fact that a new Doctor and new showrunner will arrive sooner or later and everything will change again. Bond was sort of the same - although eras tended to last much longer in the Bond franchise.

In November, MGM studio executive Pamela Abdy was asked if she knew who the next James Bond actor was going to be yet. You won't be surprised to learn that she didn't reveal the next actor (that decision was still a long way off and yet to be decided) although Abdy did say that very vague discussions on this issue had begun with Barbara Broccoli and Michael G. Wilson. Barbara Broccoli was inevitably asked about the next Bond actor during the final No Time to Die junket but by now had a long list of stock answers to deploy in order to bat off such (inevitable) inquiries. Barbara was very experienced in dealing with questions like this.

"The thing is," said Barbara, "when you cast James Bond you're not just casting one movie. You're making a decision that you're going to have to live with for at least a decade. Everybody has their own idea about what that person should be, so it's a tough decision. With Casino Royale, by deciding to do that film and follow that trajectory it made it much easier to then identify the actor to play that role. And so now we have to decide what the films are going to be like. Are they going to be more humorous or less humorous, more gritty or not gritty? And then, when we've done that, we have to figure out the actor to play it. So, no, it's not just 'Oh, who looks good in a suit?' We have to figure this out on our own."

The next Bond actor lists with bookmakers continued to be mildly comical with names like Tom Holland and Harry Styles perched near the top of the tree. Kingsman star Taron Egerton, despite short odds, seemed equally unlikely to be given the keys to Daniel Craig's Aston Martin. The closest thing to a favourite continued to be Henry Cavill. Cavill was obviously no stranger to EON because back in 2005, when he was only in his early twenties, he had tested for Casino Royale and ended up in the final three candidates alongside Daniel Craig and Sam Worthington. Henry Cavill only had a few credits (which included the film The Count of Monte Cristo) to his name at time of Casino Royale's casting. He had though a close brush with stardom in 2003 when the director McG cast him as Superman. However, McG left the film and was replaced as director by Bryan Singer. Singer cast Brandon Routh as Superman instead.

Cavill is often alleged to have been the runner up when it came to casting Bond in Casino Royale. He was definitely in there with a chance (though how much of a chance anyone else really had is open to question given that Barbara always had her heart set on Daniel Craig) until the bitter end. "Martin Campbell and I both enjoyed Henry Cavill's audition," said the former 007 composer David Arnold, who provided music for the Casino Royale screen test footage. "He had all the swagger and physicality but maybe, as he was in his early twenties, felt just a little bit too young. We thought he had great presence and we weren't at all surprised when he turned into Superman."

It is often reported that Martin Campbell wanted to cast Henry Cavill as Bond rather than Daniel Craig. It's impossible to know how true this story is but it would certainly provide an explanation for why Campbell seemed a trifle grumpy at the press conference which unveiled Craig as Bond! "Perhaps Henry Cavill was too young for it then, he was 22 at the time we auditioned for Casino Royale, but maybe he could still be James Bond in the future," Martin Campbell later said. "After all, Pierce Brosnan did a great screen test only to eventually get the part years later." When it became known that Henry Cavill was in contention to play Bond in 2005 there were rumours that Pierce Brosnan was going to come back to do Casino Royale and Cavill was going to play the younger version of Brosnan's Bond in flashbacks! These rumours were obviously nonsense. Brosnan was history.

Henry Cavill was the most traditionally 007 handsome of the Casino Royale actor candidates. There is no doubt that he looked like James Bond. Not long after his audition he was in the TV show The Tudors and in 2011 he was cast as Superman in the film Man of Steel. His status as the nearly man of Hollywood was finally put to bed. Cavill became a star in his own right. He has often spoken about his dream to play James Bond one day but it could be that 2005 was his one and only chance. "At this stage, it's all up in the air. We'll see what happens. But yes, I would love to play Bond, it would be very, very exciting," Cavill told GQ in 2020. "If Barbara and Michael were interested in that, I would absolutely jump at the opportunity."

Cavill was likely to be in his early forties by the time Bond 26 got anywhere near a start date. Was he in danger of becoming a shade too old for the part? This was a trifle ironic given that he was considered too YOUNG the last time. If anyone was an obvious person to cast as James Bond it was Henry Cavill but this, as far as his Bond aspirations were concerned, was seen as a weakness as much as it was a strength. Barbara Broccoli is not someone who is liable to go for the obvious option. As ever, Bond fans seemed slightly divided on Henry Cavill as the next James Bond. Some felt he would be terrific while others questioned his acting ability.

No Time to Die earned a decent smattering of awards from various countries. It picked up awards from the Set Decorators Society of America, the Screen Actors Guild Awards, the Art Directors Guild Awards, the Santa Barbara International Film Festival, the Japan Academy Film Prize, the Critics' Choice Super Awards, and the Houston Film Critics Society among others. EON would probably have been less pleased to see though that No Time to Die was awarded the (sarcastic) Most Egregious Age Difference Between Leading Man and Love Interest gong (thanks to Daniel Craig and Léa Seydoux playing lovers) by The Alliance of Women Film Journalists (AWFJ).

After a vigorous (if pointless Oscar) campaign by MGM, EON would doubtless have been disappointed that No Time to Die didn't get much attention when it came to the really prestigious awards. The film only got an editing award at the BAFTAS (which is Bond's home turf when it comes to the really prestigious awards ceremonies). The hope of an Oscar nomination (despite the futile campaign) proved to be predictably unrealistic. Eddie 'The Eagle' Edwards probably had more chance of winning an Olympic ski jump gold medal than No Time to Die did of getting an Oscar for best film. It didn't stop Barbara Broccoli from daydreaming about such things though. This was the difference between Barbara and Cubby. She craved awards and artistic credibility whereas

Cubby just wanted to give us a good undemanding time in the cinema for a couple of hours.

After the dust had fallen on No Time to Die, Barbara Broccoli expressed her genuine bafflement that Daniel Craig hadn't garnered a slew of acting awards for the movie. Barbara seemed blissfully unaware that an actor, however competent that actor might be, is hardly likely to be showered in prestigious acting awards for playing James Bond! You don't get Marvel executives complaining that Robert Downey Jr should be winning Oscars for playing Iron Man. Daniel Craig couldn't really complain because he'd just picked up a huge payday for No Time to Die and was about to get a star on the Hollywood walk of fame. Craig was also made an honourary officer in the Royal Navy and received the Order of St. Michael and St. George in the New Year's honours list. The Most Distinguished Order of Saint Michael and Saint George is a British order of chivalry.

In the summer of 2021, Craig had begun shooting the Knives Out sequel Glass Onion: A Knives Out Mystery. Craig was already moving on from James Bond. It was reported that he'd already signed up for Knives Out 3 and was set to earn $100 million for the two sequels. Knives Out is a 2019 detective mystery film by Rian Johnson with an all star cast. It concerns the death of the elderly Harlan Thrombey, a wealthy mystery novelist, and follows master detective Benoit Blanc (Craig) as he attempts to find out what really happened when the old man died. Matters are complicated by Thrombey's large and greedy backstabbing family - who are all naturally jostling for position in the hope that they are going to get the lion's share of the inheritance and the literary estate. The key to the mystery could well be Harley's nurse Marta Cabrera (Ana de Armas) - a woman who seems to know much more than she is letting on.

Knives Out was an enjoyable mystery caper that proved to be a huge critical and financial hit - something which had thus far been quite elusive to Craig outside of Bond. It made over $300 million from a fairly modest budget - which was enough to pave the way for a sequel. Craig seemed to be having fun as the strangely accented Benoit Blanc and unexpectedly, as his Bond tenure drew to a close, suddenly found himself with a brand new franchise. The most appealing thing about playing Benoit Blanc from Craig's point of view was that he didn't have to get smashed up doing stunts or spend months away from his family. Craig's career was doing just fine - even without the prospect of any more Bond movies in his future.

The previous Bond actors, with the obvious exception of George Lazenby, all did well outside and beyond the franchise. This would doubtless encourage Daniel Craig - not that he was shy of work anyway. Sean Connery was the most successful of all the James Bond actors outside of Bond. Largely unknown when he made Dr No, Connery mixed his James Bond days with notable appearances in films like Alfred Hitchcock's stylish Marnie. The Hill and the western Shalako saw Connery show he could play other characters - if anything Connery seemed happy and liberated to play against his Bond persona. The Anderson Tapes showed that Connery wasn't afraid to look his age and explore new roles. The Offence and Zardoz, which both followed Diamonds Are Forever, were ample proof that Connery was tired of Bond and prepared to go away from that image.

The rest of the seventies was a mixed bag for the now 007 free Connery. The Man Who Would Be King was his high point and paired him with good friend Michael Caine. Robin and Marian was an interesting if not completely successful new spin on the Robin Hood legend and the disaster film Meteor, one of his biggest duds and return to the mainstream, was a complete disaster - if you'll pardon the pun. In 1981 Connery agreed to take a small role in Terry Gilliam's Time Bandits. The film became a cult hit and restored some of Connery's star. Time Bandits reminded everyone that Connery still had great screen presence.

The High Noon inspired sci-fi film Outland gave Connery

another solid role in the same year. After making Wrong Is Right and Five Days One Summer, Connery returned as James Bond in Irvin Kershner's Never Say Never Again. The film was beaten by Octopussy at the box-office and received a mixed reception but the resulting publicity and the aura of Bond put Connery firmly back on the map. Never Say Never Again is a strange one to be sure. You could nitpick it all day and it has a lackadaisical nature that never makes it especially exciting but there are loads of moments you remember (Barbara Carrera's nutty performance, Bond shoving that chap in the broom cupboard with a gyroscope thing, the Tango, the videogame, the opening credit sequence, Edward Fox as the bad-tempered comically posh M etc). Never Say Never Again got very good reviews and gave Connery a lot of publicity.

The interesting The Name Of The Rose and the flashy but hollow Highlander continued the comeback and then Connery won an Oscar for his part in Brian De Palma's flamboyant The Untouchables. The Untouchables sealed Connery's legacy as one of his era's major film stars. Like old fashioned stars he was more or less the same in many films. Accents were never a Connery strength! His longevity as an actor confirmed, Connery had shown great skill in moving beyond James Bond. His iconic status was evident when Steven Spielberg had to cast someone as Indiana Jones' father in Indiana Jones and the Last Crusade. There was only one man for the job. The original James Bond!

The nineties was a so-so decade for Connery in terms of quality. Family Business and Just Cause gave him meaty roles but neither film was that memorable. Medicine Man and The Hunt For Red October were solid team-ups with director John McTiernan and First Knight and Dragonheart were ho-hum child friendly fodder. The Avengers bombed and the terrible Finding Forrester saw Connery giving a familiar performance as a slightly cranky mentor. The Rock was fun though.

It's a shame that the artless mauling of Alan Moore's graphic novel The League of Extraordinary Gentlemen was Connery's last film - though it must be said, even older, Connery makes for a commanding and charismatic presence in the film. He is the most respected out of all the previous Bond actors for his body of work. Connery did make a blunder near the end of his career though when he turned down the part of Gandalf in Peter Jackson's Lord of the Rings. Connery was offered 15% of the profits to play Gandalf. If he had agreed he would have made hundreds of millions of dollars.

George Lazenby, by contrast, was up a certain creek without a paddle when he quit James Bond in 1969. Wrongly advised that James Bond was finished, Lazenby sought to build a new career but quickly realised that without a CV good acting jobs are elusive. Without a background as an actor, and without the trump card of being James Bond, his career quickly slipped down the plughole. A future making Hong Kong action movies with Golden Harvest briefly beckoned after Lazenby starred in The Shrine Of Ultimate Bliss and The Man From Hong Kong. Lazenby planned to make several films with Bruce Lee and become a seventies action icon but Lee's premature death ended these plans and the Hong Kong action boom.

Lazenby, who became independently wealthy through real estate ventures, continued to pick up small parts here and there. Hawaii Five-O, General Hospital. He made a cheeky appearance as a 'James Bond type' spy in a Man From Uncle TV movie and made films with titles like Master Ninja II. Television work in the eighties included that timeless classic Baywatch, Alfred Hitchcock Presents, and Freddy's Nightmares. In 1990 he played Jor-el in Superboy. A neverending series of Emmanuelle films engaged Lazenby for much of the early nineties. Other bits and pieces included Team Knight Rider and supplying a voiceover for the Batman Beyond animated series. Perhaps Lazenby's finest post-Bond moment came when he starred with the sleuthing Van Dyke family in the mighty comedy/detective/hospital show Diagnosis Murder! Lazenby, more than any other ex-Bond, has cashed in on his Bond image for cameos and appearances. It's ironic then that he was the quickest to abandon the part.

Roger Moore was already a widely known and popular actor when he became James Bond, largely because of his television work in The Saint. A team-up with Tony Curtis in The Persuaders was fun but the series didn't last. His first non-Bond film after taking the 007 role saw him play a typically suave Roger Moore type character in Peter Hunt's adventure film Gold. Rather than seek out different roles, Roger seemed to spend most of his time outside of Bond in the seventies making some other sort of adventure film - usually with an all star cast of friends. Shout At The Devil, Escape To Athena and The Wild Geese. The Wild Geese saw Moore required to play a tougher character than usual. His character's ruthlessness in a few scenes was a contrast against his lighter Bond persona.

Moore also managed to play another iconic hero besides Bond when he starred with Patrick Macnee in a Sherlock Holmes television film. After yet another war/adventure film, The Sea Wolves, Moore had one of his more fun roles in North Sea Hijack, playing an eccentric, cat loving, counter-terrorism expert called Rufus Excalibur ffolkes. With a woollen hat and beard Moore finally began to play against his Bond image before sending it up with a cameo in the all star car chase farce The Cannonball Run.

As his Bond days drew to an end, and his work for UNICEF increased, Roger Moore appearances in films became more infrequent. He had an ill advised cameo in The Curse Of The Pink Panther and his post-Bond team up with Michael Caine in Bullseye! was notoriously bad. Films like SpiceWorld are best forgotten but Moore got a half-decent role as a caddish adventurer and conman in The Quest alongside the legend that is Jean Claude Van Damme. Bed and Breakfast, finally released in 1992, gave Moore one of his very best roles alongside Collen Dewhurst and Talia Shire. The pretty Maine seascapes gave the film an interesting backdrop and Moore showed that his charm was still there in one of his most assured performances.

Timothy Dalton wasn't widely known when he took the part of

James Bond. His CV was littered with TV miniseries parts and appearances in television shows. More than anything he was a stage actor and seemed to prefer and enjoy more varied work in that area. His West End schedule led him to decline the James Bond offer when it first arrived. He was best known for playing the dashing Prince Barin in 1981's campy cult favourite Flash Gordon. Dalton's moody good looks had led him to be cast in a number of undemanding playboy/romantic/period/ roles. Sins with Joan Collins, Florence Nightingale, and Jane Eyre. The Doctor and the Devils saw Dalton forced to don period clobber yet again.

Dalton's first film (released) outside of Bond was the well meaning but slight Hawks with Anthony Edwards. Dalton fared well in his part as a terminally ill patient who steals an ambulance and heads for Amsterdam, determined to make the best of his situation. Brenda Starr, which Dalton shot before The Living Daylights, was a complete bomb, Dalton again playing an old fashioned romantic hero character. The King's Whore showed that Dalton was unafraid to move away from the Bond persona and image, and The Rocketeer, released in 1991, gave Dalton the chance to show that he could actually be funny. Playing Neville Sinclair, a Nazi spy, Dalton had great fun and patterned his villain on Errol Flynn in this underrated and enjoyable film. A number of Bond fans noted that Dalton was engagingly dashing, funny and relaxed - traits that some had lamented as absent in Licence To Kill!

The interesting British television miniseries Framed saw Dalton play against Bond again with another morally dubious character, here alongside a young David Morrissey. Whereupon Dalton's career seemed to lose a bit of fizz. An appearance in the television series Tales From The Crypt in 1994 suggested that Dalton was treading water post-Bond and children's fare Saltwater Moose and The Beautician and The Beast confirmed that Dalton's film career was not exactly flourishing, or going anywhere interesting. More television work would follow including Rhett Butler in Scarlett and Julius Caesar in the 1999 TV movie Cleopatra.

In 2003 Dalton finally sent up his James Bond image in Looney Tunes: Back in Action. He also returned to theatre to play Lord Asriel in the stage version of His Dark Materials to great acclaim, back to where he had been most successful and fulfilled before James Bond. He had come full circle. In 2007 Dalton returned to the mainstream in Simon Pegg's Hot Fuzz. Dalton's Bond status and cult roles in films like Flash Gordon and The Rocketeer were still remembered and enjoyed by a younger generation. Dalton's renaissance continued with roles in the TV shows Penny Dreadful and Doom Patrol.

Pierce Brosnan's career was flagging when he landed James Bond. Big screen opportunities had slowed and he seemed mostly embroiled in making Alistair MacLean TV movies as UN agent Mike Graham. Graham was like James Bond without the budget and seemed to sum up where Brosnan was and simultaneously remind us that Brosnan was most famous for nearly becoming 007 once. Brosnan needed Bond big-time to jumpstart his stalled career. In 1994 he finally got the nod.

When he got the part of 007, Brosnan used his clout as Bond to carve out one of the more successful and varied careers of the ex-Bond actors. Soon he would be working with some of the famous directors going and with his own production company he was able to choose projects that interested him. After GoldenEye in 1995, Brosnan worked with Tim Burton on Mars Attacks! and played the lead in the disaster film Dante's Peak. He wasted no time in moving from the small screen back into film. John McTiernan's The Thomas Crown Affair gave Brosnan one of his better roles and cemented the fact that he was finally a star.

He followed The World Is Not Enough with John Boorman's The Tailor of Panama, a film in which he happily played against his James Bond image. Evelyn, a pet project, followed. Brosnan, like Connery before him, was able to use Bond to get films he wanted to do made. After Die Another Day, Brosnan continued with romantic comedy Laws of Attraction with Julianne Moore and After the Sunset with Woody Harrelson.

The Matador continued his move away from Bond and with the official confirmation that his services were no longer required by EON, Brosnan had entered a less lucrative but perhaps more satisfying phase of his career. Seraphim Falls illustrated that Brosnan was now old enough to attempt character roles. His career has been marked by troughs and ups and downs but Brosnan undoubtedly emerged from Bond in a much stronger position than when he went in.

As for the MI6 regulars in the Craig era, they now faced an uncertain future when it came to their participation in the franchise. Naomie Harris made no secret of the fact she'd love to come back as Moneypenny but at 45 years of age it seemed doubtful that she'd make a good fit for what was now surely going to be a much younger Bond next time around. Ralph Fiennes also said he'd be delighted to come back as M. While this was just about feasible (in the manner they brought Judi Dench back even after Brosnan was axed) it would probably be slightly odd to have him as M to a new Bond when his M had presided over the death of the previous Bond! You would presume that if Fiennes came back as M we would have to just pretend this was a different M. It might be for the best to just cast a new M. How about Idris Elba as M? Has anyone suggested that yet?

Ben Whishaw was more philosophical about his future participation and simply said that his contract was up and he would accept whatever happened. Out of these three regulars, Whishaw's Q would probably feel the least jarring to have in the next film with a fresh 007. Q, unlike Moneypenny, is a character where it doesn't matter if he's much older than Bond. Besides, Whishaw was still pretty young anyway. Whishaw suggested that Bridgerton star Jonathan Bailey should be the next Bond. Whishaw said it would be a sign of real progress to have an openly gay James Bond actor. In an interview he conducted on the eve of No Time to Die's release, Whishaw had said that, in his opinion, the Bond franchise would have to be radical and different in the future to avoid becoming a museum piece.

Rory Kinnear, who played Tanner in the Craig films, was also asked about his future participation. Kinnear said the Bond films were great fun to do and he'd never turn his back on them but did concede that it might make more sense for the next Bond actor to be surrounded with a new team to give the franchise a fresh slate. This was definitely the logical thing to do but we still didn't know yet if this would happen. Barbara would doubtless be tempted to retain actors of the calibre of Ralph Fiennes and Ben Whishaw but would have to weigh this against the needs of the next iteration of 007.

In January, Baz Bamigboye, the Daily Mail's showbusiness editor (and a man known for a few Bond scoops in his time) managed to write a short article about the future of James Bond without telling us a single thing we didn't already know. Baz told us that the next Bond would be much younger and that 49 year-old Idris Elba, despite endless newspaper clickbait connecting him to the role, was too old to be seriously considered as Daniel Craig's replacement. Bamigboye suggested that the next Bond actor would probably not be a big star and most likely have a solid theatre background. Idris Elba continued to feature so heavily in Bond articles that Barbara Broccoli was even asked about him. Barbara was forced to say that she knew Idris, thought he was great, and he was part of the conversation. This obviously did not mean that Elba was in contention. It was merely Barbara Broccoli being polite and diplomatic.

One tradition in the Bond franchise is that the director usually has some input into who the next Bond might be and also directs the audition screentests. John Glen, for example, directed a lot of Bond screentests during the Roger Moore years. When they were casting Live and Let Die they were torn over whether to cast Michael Billington or Roger Moore as the new Bond. It is alleged that Broccoli/Saltzman favoured the relatively unknown Billington (who was known for the television shows The Onedin Line and Gerry Anderson's UFO) while United Artists preferred the more famous Roger Moore. The director Guy Hamilton was given the deciding vote and went for Roger Moore. It seems most likely then that, as is custom, Bond 26 will find a director first and this director will then play an active role in helping to find the next Bond actor.

In March, it was reported that a gravestone for James Bond had been put in place on the Faroe Islands where No Time to Die did some shooting. The grave read - In Memory of James Bond, 1962–2021. The Faroese government were fully behind this ploy to attract James Bond tourists. In fact, the prime minister of the Faroes unveiled the gravestone himself. A James Bond sightseeing tour is now even available for visitors to the Faroe Islands. This illustrated the ongoing allure of Bond. Any connection to this famous character is still highly prized.

In 2022, Daniel Craig would go back on the stage to appear in Macbeth on Broadway. The producer of the play was a certain Barbara Broccoli. Some fans were a bit dismayed when they saw that Barbara was involved in this because they'd much rather she was working on Bond 26. It was unrealistic though to expect such a quick turnaround after the No Time to Die media marathon and Barbara was perfectly entitled to do other things away from James Bond. Barbara was, wisely perhaps, taking her time when it came to the next Bond film. There was still an awful lot to figure out. What tone should the post-Craig era Bond movies take? Should they be gritty or more outlandish? Who should play James Bond? Who should direct the film? Who should write the film?

EON had continued to speak very highly of Cary Fukunaga in the wake of No Time to Die and Barbara Broccoli and Michael G. Wilson both said they would love to work with him again. It didn't seem like long odds at this time to think that Fukunaga might very well be back in the director's chair for Bond 26. He even had a reboot pitch up his sleeve for such an eventuality. Allegations which mostly emerged in the summer of 2022 though would torpedo any prospect of this coming to pass. The carefully crafted image of Cary Fukunaga was now to be tarnished.

In October 2021, the actress Raeden Greer alleged that Fukunaga had fired her from a small part in his TV show True Detective several years previously because she refused to do a topless scene. Greer claimed that an angry Fukunaga, who she portrayed as a bully, put her under intense pressure to do the topless scene. When she refused, Fukunaga ruthlessly fired her and then hired an extra to do the topless scene instead. Greer said she had decided to speak up because she was absolutely disgusted to see Cary Fukunaga painting himself as some great feminist when he waxed forth about the strong women in No Time and Die and scoffed at those sexist Bond films of the past. Greer thought that Fukunaga was a big hypocrite. "And now, Cary is out here talking about his female characters," said Greer. "It's like another slap in the face over and over and over."

A woman named Rachelle Vinberg, who was in a relationship with Fukunaga which began when she was in her late teens and he was 40, was next to slate the Bond director. Vinberg said that she was always terrified of Fukunaga and that he had an unhealthy interest in much younger women. Vinberg said Fukunaga would sometimes pretend she was his sister when they went out to avoid looking like a 'predator. She portrayed Fukunaga as a very controlling, weird, and manipulative man. Vinberg's social media posts about how awful Cary Fukunaga was were liked and reposted by the actresses Margaret Qualley and Kristine Froseth - both of whom had a relationship with Fukunaga in the past.

Next in line to complain about Fukunaga were twin sisters Hanna and Cailin Loesch - who appeared in his show Maniac when they were 20. Hanna and Cailin detailed how they'd both been wooed by Fukunaga over a long period and eventually came to the conclusion that he was a bit of a creep. They allege that Fukunaga even tried tried to persuade them to have a threesome and said that incest was no big deal. Hanna and Cailin also said that during the pandemic lockdown Fukunaga showed them (the then unreleased) No Time to Die on his laptop in a bid to impress them. Fukunaga was portrayed by the twins as a spoilt middle-aged manchild who spent most of his time hanging around teenage girls.

Rolling Stone also ran an article in which former work colleagues of Fukunaga alleged that he was unprofessional and used his status in the film and television industry to manipulate young females into having a relationship with him. There were stories too that while working on Masters of the Air, crew members had noticed that Fukunaga had a creepy habit of taking photographs of young female extras as they walked to and from the set. Nick Cuse, who wrote for Fukunaga on Maniac and No Time to Die, made it clear that he supported all the women and described Fukunaga's conduct as 'horrible'. Cuse also seemed to suggest that Fukunaga was an artistic fraud who would pass off the work of other writers as his own.

'Cary Fukunaga is the worst human being I have ever met in my life,' wrote Cuse on social media. 'He didn't groom me but he did use a lot of the same tactics to get me to write his scripts for him. Which he would then put his name on. One time, after spending three weeks on a script, he made me open up the cover page and type his name under "Written By". I had to literally type the stolen credit with my own fingers. I'm ashamed to say I didn't stand up to him or say anything at the time. The worst part of the experience was that whenever someone else mentioned that a line I wrote or an idea I had was good, he would always have to change it. He couldn't bear that it was not his. Even though he was getting credit!

'As far as girls, his type is 'looks underage.' I don't know much about the things he's done to women but I'm sure they are horrible. The way he treats all people (other than celebrities) is horrible. I once saw him dump his cut fingernails in another person's car. I did not have an experience remotely comparable to [Rachelle Vinberg], [Hannah and Cailin Loesch], [Kristine Froseth]. But by speaking out, they opened my eyes to the fact that I was under the spell of a vile cult leader. If you are in the industry I hope you are aware of that before you decide to work with him. I wish someone had told me not to. I deeply regret it.'

In response to all these damaging comments from women, Cary Fukunaga's lawyer denied that he'd ever done anything wrong and said all of the relationships were consensual. Cary Fukunaga was rather hoisted by his own petard in the end. He had promoted No Time to Die as if he was the most enlightened and least sexist man in the entire world. That evidently wasn't quite the case in his real life though. The chances of Cary Fukunaga directing Bond 26 had now gone from pretty good to absolute zero.

In May, 2022, Danny Boyle was asked about his aborted Bond film in an Esquire interview. "Weirdly," said Boyle, "it would have been very topical now — it was all set in Russia, which is of course where Bond came from, out of the Cold War. It was set in present-day Russia and went back to his origins, and they just lost, what's the word... they just lost confidence in it. It was a shame really." Interestingly, Boyle said the idea of Bond having a child was from the script by John Hodge that EON jettisoned. Boyle said he would steer clear of franchises in the future and would most likely never direct a Bond film now. Boyle suggested that Paapa Essiedu or Robert Pattinson should be the next Bond. Pattinson's participation in a new Batman series made that last suggestion rather unlikely now though you would think.

In June, Barbara Broccoli and Michael G. Wilson were awarded BFI Fellowships. This prestigious honour put them in exalted company with the likes of David Lean, Michael Powell and Emeric Pressburger, and Martin Scorsese. Tim Richards, BFI Chair, said - "I am honoured and excited to be awarding Michael G. Wilson and Barbara Broccoli with the prestigious BFI Fellowship. I can think of no-one else more deserving particularly as we celebrate the 60th anniversary of the incredibly successful James Bond franchise. With amazing insight and vision Michael and Barbara have not only re-invented Bond for today's audiences, but No Time to Die arrived at exactly the right moment to welcome those audiences back to the big screen experience as never before. As equally, if not more, important is their commitment to our industry away from the spotlight, where they work tirelessly to open doors for others by playing a huge part in educating, supporting and inspiring the next generation of film makers."

Ralph Fiennes handed over the awards in person and there were video messages from Daniel Craig, Dame Judi Dench, Léa Seydoux, Rami Malek and Sam Mendes. Terry Gilliam, Edgar Wright, David Arnold, and Jamie Bell (who is occasionally mentioned as a Bond candidate - presumably because he was once in a film produced by Barbara Broccoli) were among those from the world of film who were in attendance. Barbara Broccoli was naturally asked about who the next James Bond would be (I'm pretty sure this is a question that Barbara was tired of already!) during the special evening and said that no one was in contention at all because they still had to decide what sort of approach they were going to take -let alone who they were going to cast as 007. Barbara was sensibly still keeping her cards very close to her chest when it came to Bond candidates.

The biggest problem facing Bond 26 is not really the leading man though. You should be able to find any number of actors who could make a decent fist of playing 007 and look good in a tux. The biggest problem facing Bond 26 is the usual checklist of concerns that face any new James Bond film. Coming up with new stunts. Keeping up with the action movie rivals. Coming up with a vaguely topical plot. Keeping Bond relevant. Finding a good script. Casting good actors. Finding interesting new locations. Coming up with new gadgets. And making sure the marketing campaign and release date affords the film every advantage possible when it hits the cinemas. These will be the prime concerns of Bond 26 and any Bond film you care to mention. But choosing a new 007 is always fun for the fans and media alike.

In August, 2022, it was announced that MGM had signed a

deal with Warner Bros to handle the international release of their films. This meant that Warner Bros would have an important role to play in the Bond franchise going forward. The deal did not include Bond 26 though as that would be bound by an existing deal with Universal. MGM, ever troubled by financial problems, had worked with various studios on distribution in the Craig era. Skyfall and Spectre were both made during a distribution deal with Sony. MGM had been in the Bond business since 1981. They had gained their stake in Bond through buying United Artists. With Warner Bros involved with Bond going forward and MGM now backed by Amazon's money, the 007 franchise appeared to have very firm foundations as it looked towards the future.

# CHAPTER SIX - AN ASSESSMENT OF THE CRAIG ERA

From a commercial point of view, the James Bond films made during the Daniel Craig era were undoubtedly a success. They all, to varying degrees, did more than well enough at the box-office. Skyfall in particular was a resounding financial success and made over a billion dollars - which is blockbuster status when it comes to theatrical films. The franchise ticked over very nicely during the Craig years in terms of revenue. This was aided by excellent marketing campaigns and, for the most part, fairly good reviews. The two Craig films which endured very mixed reviews were Quantum of Solace and Spectre. Casino Royale and Skyfall by contrast were universally praised. On the whole, No Time to Die did not manage to replicate the same level of critical acclaim from critics that Casino Royale and Skyfall did but, generally, it got a decent reception and much better reviews than Quantum of Solace or Spectre.

From an artistic excellence point of view, the Craig era is more difficult to judge. Casino Royale was a hard act to follow and it is debatable if the era that followed ever quite managed to build on the promise of this debut. One could say the same thing about the Brosnan years. GoldenEye was a big critical success in 1995 but the rest of the Brosnan films were fairly forgettable as far as the Bond franchise goes. If anyone were to compile their top table of James Bond films you probably wouldn't expect see films like The World Is Not Enough or Die Another Day near the top of the tree. It is no plainly coincidence that Martin Campbell directed both GoldenEye and Casino Royale - the two films which gave Brosnan and Craig respectively such a solid launch platform for their Bonds.

You would have to say that Daniel Craig got much better treatment than Brosnan from EON and the studio as far as their overall Bond tenures went. Craig got better directors, bigger budgets, more personal creative input, and more time was spent crafting his films. Craig got paid more money too - although Brosnan can't complain too much as he made $40 million from his four Bond films. One interesting factor is that Bond actors tend to get a fairly modest fee for their first Bond film and then get paid more and more each time they come back. Brosnan was paid $4 million for GoldenEye but by the time of Die Another Day he was paid £16 million. The upward pay curve of Daniel Craig was even more pronounced. Craig was paid $3 million for Casino Royale but pocketed £25 million for No Time to Die. This tradition will likely continue with the next Bond actor. They will have to do three or four films to get the really big money.

With respect to the Brosnan era directors Roger Spottiswoode, Michael Apted, and Lee Tamahori (who all did some very good work in their careers), they were clearly not the most exciting or A-list choices to direct a Bond film. Michael Apted said that after he made The World Is Not Enough he was invited to direct the next film by EON but then MGM blocked this invitation because they wanted someone of the stature of John Woo or Tony Scott to direct the next film. Guess what happened next? MGM couldn't get John Woo or Tony Scott or anyone of that ilk and Die Another Day ended up being directed by Lee Tamahori. Tamahori was definitely not an A-list Hollywood director.

In the Daniel Craig era though you got the impression that EON were pushing the boat out much more when it came to hiring top directors. Craig got Sam Mendes, Cary Fukunaga, and Marc Forster - who all arrived with a lot of artistic credibility. Thanks to the Daniel Craig era is is no longer implausible to think that someone like Christopher Nolan or Denis Villeneuve might direct a James Bond film one day. You could say then that the Craig era gave the franchise more artistic integrity when it came to its allure for big directors. The experimental nature of the Craig era is a factor in this. If you direct a Bond film now you probably expect to be given a bit more leeway when it comes to probing the conventions of the formula. You aren't just a hired hand who is expected to churn out a Tomorrow Never Dies.

The films featuring Daniel Craig patently benefited by a more consistent tone than those starring Brosnan. Though the often morose 'gritty' Bond essayed by Craig was definitely not everyone's cup of tea and probably outstayed its welcome in the end, it was resolute in its determination to venture down this path right until the bitter end. No Time to Die was definitely not out to give you an undemanding good time! You might argue that, out of the Craig films, Spectre was a trifle more breezy but it was hardly Moonraker all the same.

The Brosnan films clearly suffered from a confused tonal approach. The World is Not Enough (despite the presence of Denis Richards as a nuclear physicist!) tried to inject a modicum of drama and realism but then you get Die Another Day with its ice palaces and invisible cars. The tone of the Brosnan era is all over the place. They can't decide if they want him to be Sean Connery, Timothy Dalton or Roger Moore. He ends up being like a sort of composite of all the Bonds that have come before. This is a shame because the one reliable constant in that era was Brosnan himself. He was always good but after GoldenEye never quite got the 007 movie he deserved. A fantastical Brosnan Bond film was there for the taking but a shoddy, not to mention eccentric, script compromised Die Another Day. That Pierce managed to keep his head above water in the chaos of Die Another Day is a testament to his onscreen presence. The film did boffo business at the time though. $175 million in the US alone. Not so long ago they could only have dreamed of those figures.

Die Another Day is the film which led to the fresh slate reboot featuring Daniel Craig. What was so bad about Die Another Day? The bad would have to include the story - especially the North Korean angle, the innuendo driven dialogue, the horrible CGI (which afflicts many films of this era), slightly overlong mechanical action scenes, and the annoying Toby Stephens as Graves. Halle Berry wasn't helped either by the character she was asked to play or some of her lines. The somewhat thrown together climax of Die Another Day features Bond and Jinx on a huge transport plane where Graves has a Robocop style suit. Lee Tamahori admitted making up this sequence because they didn't have an ending and I think we all believe him. The CGI was a low point in the series. If the para-surfing ice glacier stunt couldn't have been shot with real people it should've been shelved. We need Bond believably in the thick of the action - not cut scenes from MSDOS games.

One big advantage that Craig had over Brosnan is that he had much more creative input into the films. Craig had approval of directors and scripts. Brosnan patently did not enjoy any of these advantages. If he had been allowed to personally choose his own directors then it is highly doubtful that Brosnan would have approved the likes of Michael Apted or Lee Tamahori. He'd have been more likely to be on the telephone to personal friends like John McTiernan and Renny Harlin. Despite all the high-brow bluster that surrounded the Craig era though he did have his own little mini disaster in the form of Quantum of Solace. This film seems to have picked up some fans on Bond forums but in 2008 it got a lot of brickbats and even suggested the reboot might have already hit the buffers.

Quantum of Solace is the 22nd James Bond and the second to feature Daniel Craig in the lead role. Fleming's short story Quantum of Solace has nothing in common with the 2008 film. The short story has Bond dining with the Governor of the Bahamas and listening to a yarn about an airline attendant. Although Ian Fleming never wrote a direct continuation novel to Casino Royale, EON decided to have a crack themselves of sorts and the film follows straight on from the events of 2006's Casino Royale. In fact, as was custom in the Craig era, some sort of knowledge of that film is a distinct help when viewing this film for the purposes of character motivation and the ability to recognise characters who return.

Quantum Of Solace sees Bond tangle with villain Dominic Greene (Mathieu Amalric), a spurious environmentalist who wants to stage a coup in Bolivia to gain control of the water supplies. No, he's not exactly Auric Goldfinger but there you go. Greene is a member of the 'Quantum Organisation', a mysterious new group that MI6 and Bond are eager to find out more about. The 'Quantum Organisation' is a very tacked-on invention by the writers not a Fleming creation, the name presumably chosen to make some sort of connection between the title and the film. I don't actually mind the title myself but I can understand non Fleming fans were somewhat perplexed by it. It takes a bit of getting used to I suppose. It's really an attempt to go back to a SPECTRE type group, SPECTRE being unavailable at the time to EON through the combined efforts of Kevin McClory and Austin Powers, although the group is vague to the extreme in Quantum Of Solace. You wouldn't have missed them if they hadn't bothered.

Very early in the film Mr White (Jesper Christensen), the man shot and captured by Bond at the end of Casino Royale, mocks both M and Bond in an interrogation scene about how little they know, hinting that Quantum has people in high places. As they were implicated in the death of Vesper Lynd, it prompts Bond to investigate them for himself, leading to a tremendous body-count Michael Myers would be proud of and an endless barrage of rapidly edited action sequences.

Quantum Of Solace has no gunbarrel sequence at the beginning of the film. The iconic staple that puts the audience in the Bond mood is sadly absent again. It turns up elsewhere and isn't done very well. We then move into an ear-splitting car chase in Italy with Bond being pursued in his Aston Martin by countless other cars. It is reminiscent of the chase at the end of the second Bourne film with the speeded up comic book style of The Transporter films but is far too rapidly cut and confusing, ending up on some sort of quarry. The beginning of the film also has sweeping vistas of sea and mountains intercut a bit like the opening sequence to The Big Blue. This will be Marc Forster, the film's arty Swiss director trying to make himself heard over the second-unit stunt crew who have taken over the film.

The title sequence for Quantum Of Solace is a great disappointment. The song 'Another Way To Die' by Jack White is just absolutely awful and charmless and Daniel Kleinman, who, in the absence of such names as Ken Adam, John Barry, Maurice Binder and Derek Meddings, was the most talented person left on the EON payroll, was elbowed by director Marc Forster in favour of design company MK12. Their title sequence is bland and unmemorable with dull desert shots and crude cartoon images. The film proper wastes no time in cutting to the mayhem with locations including Haiti, Austria and the desert - all given to us onscreen with a pointlessly arty font.

In 1997's Tomorrow Never Dies, script problems resulted in large portions of the film being written or rewritten as they entered production. The result was a surfeit of action sequences that meant the film became mechanical. It seems that similar problems affected Quantum Of Solace - which had a similar situation in that its original script was dumped prior to production. Quantum Of Solace doesn't have much of a plot and, without an Ian Fleming book to work from, EON clearly struggled with the film clocking in a whopping forty minutes shorter than Casino Royale. Given this it's astonishing that such a short film is packed with so many hollow action sequences. A bit of plot and coherence in place of the weaker set-pieces would have clearly helped.

Another weakness is that just when most of the (older) Bond films are setting up a big ending this one abruptly begins to end. The Bourne influence in Quantum Of Solace is very apparent. Indeed, there are three or four sequences that could have been lifted straight out that that rival spy series. A fight in a hotel room which, while striving to bring a brutal air into Bond, plays like a carbon copy of a scene in The Bourne Identity. A rooftop chase which is again cut in a very eccentric fashion and reminds one of The Bourne Ultimatum. Bond seemed to be constantly chasing or killing somebody in Quantum of Solace and half the time you have no idea why.

Even shots of Craig on a motorbike (going comically slowly) remind you of the (former) amnesiac, American spy. The absurd decision not to use the famous James Bond music, apart from a few bars here and there, doesn't help the film either. It's the whole Bond experience and a modicum more wit, fun and charm that is missing in Quantum of Solace. There are not enough witty lines in the film for any of the characters as the action continues to pile up.

There is a speedboat chase that doesn't really work and a section set at a performance of Tosca at Lake Constance with shots of Bond shooting countless people in some sort of arty slo-mo John Woo impersonation, intercut with the opera a la The Godfather III. Incredibly, there is more mayhem to come, including Bond avoiding a SWAT team who shoot up a bar and an aeroplane sequence which was done better in The Living Daylights. This section is marred by an implausible parachute drop which actually begins begins to approach the giddy lows of the para-surfing CGI in Die Another Day. That is one of the other problems with this film. It strives to be gritty, even grainy at times (Bond even meets M in a London sink estate tower block) but Daniel Craig, who was hired for his acting, is made to appear the most superhumanly invulnerable Bond ever at times in some of the more improbable and many action sequences that are sent his way.

Halfway through one of these endless bursts of action you suddenly realised the film was wrapping up. One doesn't even realise that we were approaching some sort of resolution! What of the cast in Quantum Of Solace? Well Mathieu Amalric as Dominic Greene hardly registers. One was never quite sure what he was doing and it seems we've barely been introduced to him before he's tackling Bond in the climax. Olga Kurylenko's South American agent Camille Montes hooks up with Bond for much of the film as they both seek revenge on Quantum. Kurylenko doesn't have much acting range or chemistry with Daniel Craig but she throws herself into the action as best she can.

Gemma Arterton, a capable actress, is wasted as MI6 agent Fields. Saddled with the worst Bond girl haircut since Teri Hatcher in Tomorrow Never Dies, she has precious little screen time and a ludicrous character to play. Why would M send a young woman to bring back Bond? He kills half the planet in this film! The expanded role of Judi Dench as M here is very welcome. This is a very incoherent film and she brings a brief air of calmness and authority whenever she appears. Jeffrey Wright as Felix Leiter is another plus although his nice line in jovial dryness is at odds with this helter-skelter and sometimes grim nature of this film.

Overall, Quantum Of Solace is a strangely uninvolving film, rattling along with endless second-unit action. You sense that a better film was lost in a London editing room. Bits it of look good but it hardly delivers on the promise to evoke the look and feel of the great Ken Adam. The new space age MI6 headquarters with touch screen computers smacks more of a way-out Pierce Brosnan entry and doesn't really fit the tone of Quantum Of Solace. The film is also not shy of a homage/rip-off or too, like the much maligned Die Another Day, with Moonraker, Goldfinger, and The Man With The Golden Gun all providing 'inspiration' here in one form or another.

Quantum Of Solace also has a hint of a rape scene and one or two crude lines. There is little of the panache of the Bond Fleming created here or the charm of the cinematic Bond. Fleming's Bond disliked killing and Fleming said Bond should never be drunk. Well, he's drunk in this film and it makes the character seem like just any other person. This scene is also made incredibly annoying by a barman, for reasons which escape me, reading out the ingredients of the 'Vesper' Martini.

Although the film looks sleek at times, it's all surface slickness. Quantum Of Solace steams along with the earnest vacuity and hollow motivation of one of those Matrix sequels, all the while trying desperately to be Jason Bourne, with little or no story. Casino Royale director Martin Campbell was brutally honest when he was asked what he thought of Marc Forster's follow-up movie Quantum of Solace. "Oh, I thought it was lousy," said Campbell. "I just thought the story was pretty uninteresting. I didn't think the action was related to the characters. I just thought overall it was a bit of a mess really."

EON were able to offer something of a course correction after Quantum of Solace by making Skyfall. This film, which had more time to be crafted, managed to hire the Oscar winning director Sam Mendes. Skyfall, which had Bond presumed dead but then returning to battle ghosts from his past, was hugely successful with both critics and at the box-office. The reason why Skyfall worked and Quantum of Solace didn't was that Skyfall had a concept underpinning its story.

Sam Mendes decided to have Bond's age be a part of the story. So, the Bond in Skyfall is feared to be past his prime and damaged goods and has to essentially prove himself all over again. Skyfall also brought back Q and Moneypenny and hired some big talented names like Javier Bardem and Ralph Fiennes to put alongside Daniel Craig. Skyfall is definitely an odd film at times but it is also a confident film because it knows exactly what it wants to do. Skyfall also got a lot of marketing hype due to the fact that it was Judi Dench's last film as M and there was a lot of (eventually verified) speculation that she was going to be killed off.

The lack of a clear concept was apparent though when Sam Mendes returned for Spectre. In this movie, on a mission in Mexico, Bond comes into the possession of an octopus ring after killing criminal Sciarra (Alessandro Cremona). When he skirts the funeral of Sciarra he meets his widow Lucia (Monica Bellucci) and learns about a shadowy and dangerous criminal organisation. You may guess where this is all heading. That octopus ring will be useful. Back in London, the Double O Section is under threat from the shifty Max Denbigh (Andrew Scott). Denbigh plans a new "Nine Eyes" intelligence structure involving eight other countries. M is not too chuffed about this and begins a power struggle with Denbigh. Bond, for his part, meets the ailing Mr White and then meets up with White's daughter Madeleine Swann, a psychologist in the Alps.

There is more humour in Spectre than the previous three Craig films. Think of the moment in The Spy Who Loved Me when Roger Moore hands the bystander on the beach a fish as he drives off in his Lotus. I don't even know how to describe what Moore did there but it's funny. The same with Brosnan when he stops and looks at Wai Lin walking up the wall in Tomorrow Never Dies. They give Daniel Craig some of this shtick in Spectre. The cinematography by Hoyte van Hoytema is interesting and the film has some atmosphere in places, like the initial Alpine scenes. The scene where Bond infiltrates a SPECTRE meeting for the first time whips up some intrigue. Ben Whishaw is likeable too. Q has a bigger part this time because Whishaw can act and he's quite good at comedy but poor Moneypenny though is shunted to the background.

Christoph Waltz hardly has any screen time in Spectre and his over-mannered acting style is distracting. You'd think that Waltz as a Bond villain would be amazing but he can't work any miracles with the script. If EON knew they were going to get the rights to use SPECTRE they probably wouldn't have invented the Quantum Organisation. There's some farcical retconning as a consequence. SPECTRE was behind Quantum and everything that has happened to James Bond in the last three films. It's like a soap opera when they suddenly introduce a pivotal relative who has never been mentioned in the previous 967 episodes. They probably should have held SPECTRE back and not jumped the gun in using them straight away.

Spectre is a fairly middle of the road Craig entry. Critics (especially in the United States) gave it quite a rough ride at times but it isn't a palpably bad film in the way that Quantum of Solace is. Spectre is decent enough at times - although the last act where the MI6 team rattle around London and Blofeld crashes a helicopter into a bridge feels rather desperate and on the fly. The Craig films were heavily influenced by Bourne at their inception but Spectre is one of the most evident signs that they are now being influenced by the Mission Impossible films (a franchise which seems to get better and better the longer it goes on).

The worst thing about Spectre is the silly twist where Bond and Blofeld are revealed to have been step-brothers. The Blofeld family connection twist is one of the dumbest ideas to appear in a Bond film. It should have been torpedoed the moment it was even suggested. This twist is vaguely connected to Fleming. Octopussy and The Living Daylights was the final James Bond offering by Ian Fleming and published posthumously in 1966. A slim volume, the first story Octopussy concerned a murder victim named Oberhauser found frozen in an Austrian glacier. James Bond is personally involved in the case as Oberhauser was a mentor to him after the death of his parents. "It just happened that Oberhauser was a friend of mine. He taught me to ski before the war, when I was in my teens. He was a wonderful man. He was something of a father to me at a time when I happened to need one." This Fleming story is the flimsy basis for some ludicrous retroactive continuity in Spectre.

Although Skyfall made more money and got slightly better reviews, most people would probably contend that Casino

Royale was the best film of the Craig era. This picture was obviously aided considerably by the fact that it had an Ian Fleming novel to use as the basis for its story. The film was also overseen by the reliable Martin Campbell. Campbell seems to have a better intuitive grasp for Bond than other contemporary directors in the franchise. Sam Mendes got a lot of plaudits for Skyfall but you wouldn't necessarily say that Mendes was a natural fit for Bond or that he understood it perfectly. The series had to change to accommodate Mendes. Campbell, on the other hand, just seems to have a good instinct for Bond and his Bond films never feel as if too much has had to change.

Not to say Campbell's films are perfect. One can argue that GoldenEye is a bit overrated. Some of the scenes at the MI6 HQ in London and some of the early Russian sequences could have been cut to give the film a better flow. GoldenEye does seem a bit jumbled at times and Eric Serra's sparse score isn't a huge plus. Serra was a bold and interesting choice after his work for Luc Beeson but it didn't quite come off and he seemed to go to great lengths to avoid using the James Bond music. Personally, if I watch a James Bond film I want the James Bond theme!

All of this is mitigated though in GoldenEye by a general sense of fun that runs through the whole film with many entertaining moments. The pre-credit sequence, the Aston/Ferrari chase, a scene where Bond derails a train belonging to the villains and a terrific climax set around a huge satellite dish located in the middle of a jungle. In fact, with GoldenEye, Martin Campbell probably pulled off to date, the last really grand-scale fun climax to a 007 film. There is also an excellent close quarter fight between 007 and 006 at the end that is very well done and edited for extra punch.

All the Bond eras have been influenced, by varying degrees, to prevailing trends and fads or things from the past. The Sean Connery films took some inspiration from Hitchcock and Saturday morning cliffhanger serials. The Hitchcock film that the Connery films were most inspired by is North By Northwest. One of the most famous scenes in North By Northwest occurs at 'Prairie Stop Highway 41' when Cary Grant's Thornhill is lured to an isolated location surrounded by huge cornfields with a long lonely road for company. We (and Thornhill) notice a crop-dusting plane gradually coming too close for comfort until it becomes apparent that the plane is after Thornhill himself.

This famous Hitchcock set-piece was clearly a big inspiration for a similar scene in the James Bond film From Russia With Love and Roger Thornhill's adventures were assuredly an influence on the early Bond pictures. Both North By Northwest and the James Bond films feature some interesting parallels in that both are glamorous travelogues with high-living sophisticated characters matching wits and feature enigmatic, beautiful women who may or may not be trustworthy. Plus, of course, explosions and stunts and set-pieces at famous locations and landmarks, suggestive dialogue banter, dry quips from an urbane, witty villain, and double-dealing and spying in general with a 'vital' object (MacGuffin) thrown out there to supply plot and character motivation.

As the restrictions on sex and violence began to loosen, the James Bond series gave sixties audiences an irresistible cocktail of glamour, exotic locales, humour, suspense, stunts and scantily clad women. The formula, perfectly encapsulated by Goldfinger in 1963, placed a suave man of action against various eccentric, colourful villains. The modern action film was born and espionage became a common theme in cinema. To be inspired by or borrow from things that may have been inspired elsewhere is common but in the action/adventure genre all things usually lead back to 007. Of course there were spy and adventure pictures before 007 but the James Bond franchise took the elements into the modern age and spawned countless imitators.

During the spy craze period of the mid-1960s it seemed that nearly every show borrowed elements from the James Bond series. Espionage-themed television programmes included I Spy, Mission Impossible, The Man From U.N.C.L.E., Get Smart, and Danger Man. Shows like the Prisoner and The Avengers incorporated a fantasy element into the mix. The Avengers was about the urbane bowler hatted John Steed (Patrick Macnee) - a government agent for the 'Ministry' who battled various villains in some often bonkers and surreal plots. Steed's female agent partners in the show were Cathy Gale (Honor Blackman), then Emma Peel (Diana Rigg), and finally Tara King (Linda Thorson).

Although Honor Blackman did it all first, it is Diana Rigg as Emma Peel who is most associated with the heyday of the show, her playful banter with Patrick Macnee and leather catsuits making her something of an icon in the decade. The arrival of Rigg ushered in the most iconic and famous period for the show and her double act with Patrick Macnee (and general elegance and poise as she sipped champagne and karate chopped villains) helped the series to go from strength to strength. It became a hit in America and was shot on film - adding an even more stylish gloss to the wonderful costumes and sets. Blackman and Rigg would become two of the most famous and memorable Bond Girls.

On television, Roger Moore starred as the suave troubleshooter Simon Templar. Ian Ogilvy later also filled the role on TV in the seventies. Simon Dutton and Andrew Clarke (an Australian actor who tested to play Bond for The Living Daylights) both later played Templar in largely forgotten television projects. The later Val Kilmer film effort, which was planned as a series, is best forgotten. Although not a spy in the strictest sense of the word, Templar is an enigmatic figure, living under assumed names and with a shady history - his services can be bought and sold, he is against violence, and he can assume any identity. Roger Moore's charm in the role of Templar kept him in the 007 sweepstakes long enough to nab the role in the early seventies.

The sixties definitely went spy mad in pop culture. The

Manchurian Candidate was a 1959 thriller novel written by Richard Condon, later adapted into films in 1962 and 2004. The first and best of these starred starred Frank Sinatra, Laurence Harvey, Angela Lansbury and Janet Leigh. Raymond Shaw is perhaps the most effective type of spy - an agent who doesn't realise that he is working at all, having been programmed by the government to carry out their bidding. A big-screen counterpoint to the 007 series featured Michael Caine as the bespectacled, world-weary Harry Palmer - developed for the screen by Bond producer Harry Saltzman.

Palmer was devised by Len Deighton in his series of novels. He got a series of sorts with The Ipcress File, Funeral in Berlin and Billion Dollar Brain. Stylish and well-made, with distinctive music, the films are well worth seeking out if you haven't seen all of them. Whereas Sean Connery's agent was lavishly equipped with ingenious gadgets, visited numerous exotic sun-drenched locales, frequently wore a tuxedo and saved the world on a regular basis in a total fantasy environment with absolute loyalty to Queen and Country, Harry Palmer was a downbeat, cynical, anti-authoritarian spy who wore thick NHS specs, shopped in supermarkets and munched on cornflakes.

It was a clever move to go in a radically different direction by Saltzman and subsequently the Palmer series exists on its own terms as an intelligent and interesting series of films rather than leave itself too open to the charge of being a Bond clone in an era that was festooned with them. The emphasis here is on a more downbeat, film noir detective atmosphere and while James Bond is a playboy of sorts, an urbane expense account snob and former Royal Navy Commander who had a private education, Harry Palmer is an ordinary Joe, working off a two-year sentence for black market activities he undertook in Berlin once.

1964's Carry On Spying was naturally inspired by the incredible success of the Cubby Broccoli/Harry Saltzman produced James Bond films. The Carry On series began in

1958 and released regular films until 1978. It was resurrected in 1992 but that venture (Carry On Columbus) proved that the series belonged to the fifties and - especially - the sixties and seventies and should probably remain there. The films, produced by Peter Rogers on very modest budgets and directed by the unflappable Gerald Thomas (who often managed to get scenes done with one take to save time and money), span out of the British tradition of saucy seaside postcards and music hall. Double entendres and innuendo.

Though critics were sniffy, audiences loved the films and they often featured in the top ten domestic box-office hits of the year. The Carry Ons were a uniquely British institution (Peter Rogers was proud of the fact that they didn't use any foreign money to fund them). One of the secrets of the success behind the series was the stock company that formed around them. Sid James, Kenneth Williams, Charles Hawtrey, Joan Sims, Hattie Jacques, Peter Butterworth, Kenneth Connor etc. These were not out and out comedians but rather actors who had the ability to play comedy. It was an important difference and the reason why they were chosen.

Carry On Spying is an enjoyable romp that has fun lampooning the gadget festooned nature of the Bond films with the team a bunch of often incompetent spies. There are also riffs on The Third Man in addition to Ian Fleming's superspy. Peter Rogers later recalled how he was badgered by Harry Saltzman's lawyer after rumours that Charles Hawtrey was going to be called 001½ in the film. Rogers claims that he dumped the prefix but stood his ground when EON even objected to the name "Bind" being used in the film.

An American version of 'Harry Palmer' with a Harold Pinter screenplay from the first of Adam Hall's many Quiller novels - was Quiller. An agent (George Segal) is called upon by Alec Guinness to infiltrate neo-Nazis (led by Max von Sydow) in post-war Berlin in The Quiller Memorandum (1966). Would be rival Bonds of the sixties included Matt Helm and Derek Flint. Helm starred in thirty novels by Donald Hamilton and the government operative got to the big screen when Columbia pictures decided to jump onto the Bond craze. In a move that probably didn't please all Helm fans, the pictures were spoofs with a slightly sozzled looking Dean Martin lending his laid-back style to proceedings. The Silencers (1966), Murderer's Row (1966), The Ambushers (1967), and The Wrecking Crew (1968) are sporadically entertaining but laissez faire with the source material.

Our Man Flint is a fun 1966 tongue-in-cheek spy adventure directed by Daniel Mann that attempts to both parody and beat James Bond at his own game. The wealthy and urbane playboy Derek Flint (James Coburn) is an impossibly suave, sophisticated and brilliant secret agent and former employee of Z.O.W.I.E. - Zonal Organization World Intelligence Espionage. When three nutty rogue scientists - Doctor Krupov (Rhys Williams), Doctor Wu (Peter Brocco), and Doctor Schneider (Benson Fong) - from a SPECTRE type organisation known as "Galaxy" use advanced technology to gain control of the weather they hold the world to ransom with eco-terrorism, threatening earthquakes, volcano mayhem and obstreperous storms.

With the best trained secret agents of intelligence organisations suddenly being killed around the world at an alarming rate, the Zen like Flint, a martial artist, scientist, and expert in languages, including Russian and Dolphin!, is empirically selected for the mission by a giant high-tech super computer - much to the chagrin of his former Z.O.W.I.E. boss Lloyd Cramden (Lee J Cobb). "Very well gentlemen," he sighs. "Flint it is." An initially reluctant Flint is finally persuaded to come out of retirement to tackle this dastardly threat after a pre-emptive assassination attempt on his life by Galaxy's section head Gila (Gila Golan) which nearly kills Cramden. "I'm going to put Galaxy into orbit," promises our hero.

Our Man Flint is possibly the cheekiest of the Bond clones in that this is for all intents and purposes a James Bond film where James Bond just happens to be an American and called

Derek Flint. Granted, Flint is even more knowingly, winkingly implausible than the more lavish gilt-edged sixties Bonds, but no attempt is made to hide the inspiration for this enjoyable piece of fluffy sixties nonsense. The guiding principle behind the film is that whatever James Bond can do Derek Flint can do too, only more so. The film was well received but 1967's In Like Flint seemed to stretch the joke a bit too far. Derek Flint was more or less done although he, perhaps as much as Bond, inspired Mike Myers one-joke Austin Powers series. Ray Danton later played Flint in a 1976 television pilot.

A secret agent named Hubert Bonnisseur de la Bath alias O.S.S. 117, was created by French thriller novelist Jean de Bruce; the character was a wealthy Louisiana gentleman who spied for the American OSS, and was found in a number of films (pre- and post-Bond) popular with European audiences: OSS 117 Is Not Dead (1956, Fr) (aka OSS 117 N'Est Pas Mort), O.S.S. 117: Double Agent (1967) and No Roses For OSS 117 (1968, Fr) (aka Pas De Roses Pour OSS 117) - both with John Gavin as the agent. John Gavin of course almost become James Bond at a later date. 2006 saw the release of OSS 117: Cairo, Nest of Spies (OSS 117: Le Caire nid d'espions), a spoof of the earlier series and Bond films. Jean Dujardin took the lead role for the update and further O.S.S 117 adventures are planned.

For many years, Casino Royale was the one Ian Fleming novel that had always managed to escape the clutches of EON. In the sixties - while Albert R Broccoli and Harry Saltzman were busy with their immensely lucrative series featuring Sean Connery - it was rival producer Charles Feldman who held the screen rights to Ian Fleming's original James Bond book. Rather envious of the incredible success the Bond franchise had enjoyed, Feldman set out to make a parody of the Broccoli/Saltzman series. The end result was a legendary disaster and a chaotic production that went through six directors and countless writers. A headache-inducing mess that Woody Allen, roped into proceedings as an actor (with his proposed six weeks in London for the shoot ending up closer to six months), had little time for and later described as 'moronic'.

To make matters worse, one of the principle stars of Casino Royale, Peter Sellers, walked out on the project halfway through, leaving Feldman and a revolving door of directors and writers desperately trying to salvage a completed film from the wreckage. The plot of Casino Royale, released in 1967 by Columbia Pictures, revolves around the retired 'Sir' James Bond, played by David Niven (who ironically was one of Ian Fleming's favoured choices to become first big screen 007 in 1962's Dr No and also mentioned by name in the novel The Spy Who Loved Me). The film makes clear that this is the 'real' James Bond with one or two jokes about Connery's Bond being some sort of codename replacement. "That sexual acrobat who leaves a trail of dead beautiful women like so many blown roses behind him, that bounder to whom you gave my name and number."

In this version of Casino Royale, British, American and Russian agents are being murdered and the heads of the world's secret services decide to call the real James Bond out of retirement to find those responsible. Bond refuses at first but after an explosion at his house accounts for M and a visit to M's ancestral castle in Scotland reveals it has been infiltrated by SMERSH, he takes over as the head of the secret service and, to confuse the enemy, renames all British agents James Bond 007. As far as psychedelic sixties capers go Casino Royale is overblown and ultimately just a bit dull and leaden. While it has a nice soundtrack and some inventive futuristic sets the film just isn't consistently funny enough and the lack of coherence eventually makes the picture tiresome. If you like swinging sixties escapism you'd have a lot more fun watching Barbarella or one of those Derek Flint films with James Coburn instead.

Richard Johnson featured in the resurrected role of British agent Bulldog Drummond (a suave, gentleman-spy hero in many films mostly made between the silents through to the late 40s) in Deadlier Than the Male (1967) and Some Girls Do (1969). Johnson also featured in 1967's Danger Route. Danger Route was directed by Seth Holt and written by Meade Roberts and Robert Banks Stewart. It was based on Andrew York's 1966 novel The Eliminator. Although Amicus Productions was a horror studio they would occasionally try something out of their usual comfort zone. One such film was Danger Route, an espionage thriller made at the height of the sixties spy craze. Richard Johnson plays British spy Jonas Wilde. Jonas wants to retire but is told he can only resign if he does one last mission.

This mission involves killing a Czech defector who is in the custody of the Americans. Jonas manages to complete his mission but then becomes aware that his superior has vanished and British agents are being murdered. There seems to be a traitor or some sort of double-cross at play. Jonas resolves to get the bottom of this knotty espionage mystery. This is a strange sort of film that positions itself somewhere in the gulf between the high fantasy Bond films and more down to earth and gritty Harry Palmer series with Michael Caine. You'd say though that Danger Route is much closer to Harry Palmer than it is to the likes of Goldfinger and Thunderball. It is certainly something of an irony that Richard Johnson turned down the part of James Bond in Dr No but then spent much of the decade making spy films!

Neil Connery (Sean Connery's brother) appeared in a dreadful Italian action-spy film titled Operation Kid Brother (1967) (aka O.K. Connery) which also featuring perennial Bond characters Bernard Lee and Lois Maxwell (although not identified as M or Miss Moneypenny). This film is pretty awful and its mere existence apparently irritated Sean Connery a great deal. When Eight Bells Toll (1971) was adapted from Alistair MacLean's bestselling book, and set in the Scottish Highlands, with Anthony Hopkins in a Bond-like role (Hopkins is sort of like Craig's Bond in this film in that he is a no nonsense type of spy) as Philip Calvert in a search for missing/stolen government gold bullion. Le Magnifique (1973,

Fr.) (aka How to Destroy the Reputation of the Greatest Secret Agent in the World), was a spy-comedy parody of the James Bond films, starring Jean Paul Belmondo.

The films in the Roger Moore era of Bond took inspiration from a raft of places. There is some Blaxsploitaion and voodoo horror in Live and Let Die and some Hong Kong kung fu in the Man with the Golden Gun. This latter film took a bit of inspiration from the 007 inspired Enter the Dragon - which is surely one of the best Bond inspired action films ever made. Enter the Dragon is a classic 1973 Hong Kong based martial arts film directed by Robert Clouse and starring Bruce Lee. Lee (known simply as Lee in the film also) plays a Shaolin monk and martial arts expert sequestered by intelligence bigwig Braithwaite (Geoffrey Weeks) to investigate the dealings of the mysterious and highly dubious Han (Kien Shih).

A high-energy action film with great fight sequences, Enter the Dragon is somewhat dated of course but the camp seventies trappings are a lot of fun to modern eyes and there is much to enjoy here. Enter the Dragon plays like a low-budget James Bond at times but also stands as perhaps the seminal martial arts picture and a perfect showcase for the physical dexterity of its much missed star - who sadly died at just 33 years of age not long after the completion of the film. The film is good fun when the action switches to Han's private island and we meet Betty Chung as Mei Ling, Lee's inside contact.

There is a real James Bond feel to Enter the Dragon at times as Lee and the other guests are wined and dined in lavish fashion and he eventually slips out of his quarters late at night in the type of black secret operative clobber that Sean Connery had over the top of his tuxedo in the PTS of Goldfinger. Lee deploys climbing ropes to clandestinely infiltrate the inner echelons of Han's operations and complex and this is all highly enjoyable.

Han is obviously a James Bond villain with his secret base, private island, penchant for calling people by their surnames, musings on his unique line of work - "We are investing in corruption, Mr Roper. The business of corruption is like any other business!" - metal hand (pure Ian Fleming), and urbane and civilised exterior which, of course, hides a complete and utter nutcase up to all sorts of nonsense. "Gentlemen, welcome," charms Han. "You honour our island. I look forward to a tournament of truly epic proportions. We are unique, gentlemen, in that we create ourselves. Through long years of rigorous training, sacrifice, denial, pain, we forge our bodies in the fire of our will. But tonight, let us celebrate. Gentlemen, you have our gratitude." Han even has a classic Bond villain speech when he talks about how Sparta, Rome, The Knights of Europe, and the Samurai flourished because they worshipped strength.

The era of Roger Moore's 007 was also influenced by Star Wars, 2001, and Indiana Jones. Indiana Jones is the greatest of all the Bond inspired heroes and first came to the screen in 1981's Raiders Of The Lost Ark. Adventurer/archaeologist Indiana Jones is inspired by James Bond, cliffhanger serials and Gunga Din. The character began life in a vague treatment George Lucas had first drafted in the early seventies. He eventually went off to do Star Wars instead but the project resurfaced again several years later when his friend Steven Spielberg was snubbed by United Artists and Cubby Broccoli after he asked if he could direct a James Bond film. Lucas told him he had something that was like James Bond but even better.

George Lucas saw Indiana Jones as a James Bondish playboy adventurer but Spielberg wanted the hero more rough around the edges and down to earth. The compromise worked out well enough and Indiana Jones emerged as a very American almost blue collar fusion of Bond and Alan Quatermain. Indy, like Bond in the sixties, spawned his own copycats. High Road To China, King Soloman's Mines, Romancing The Stone, Jewel Of The Nile, Jake Speed, Big Trouble In Little China, The Phantom and The Mummy all attempted to ride on his coattails with varying degrees of success.

Remo Williams: The Adventure Begins was released in 1985 and planned as a Bond style series. The action/adventure film featured Fred Ward, Joel Grey and Kate Mulgrew. It was directed by James Bond veteran Guy Hamilton with input from Christopher Wood. The character was based on The Destroyer pulp paperback series. The film however didn't catch on and Remo's big-screen adventures came to an abrupt halt. It can only be a matter of time before someone has another stab at Remo.

Jake Speed, a low-budget Indiana Jones derivative, promised a return to the sleek screen-hero in an era of Arnie and Sly but the film was too low-rent to ever take off. They did somehow manage to rope Denis Christopher and John Hurt in though. John Carpenter's Big Trouble In Little China was billed as the first in a possible James Bond style series for the lead character Jack Burton, a truck driver with a John Wayne swagger who always ends up in big trouble. The film however, as gloriously enjoyably fun as it is, bombed at the box-office.

The eighties Jackie Chan films, when he was in his Hong Kong heyday, certainly took some inspiration from the Bond franchise. A film worth watching is Chan's Armour of God - which is like an enjoyable cross between Bond and Indiana Jones. Chan would later make some more overtly Bondian films in his later Hollywood phase but these were never as good.

John MacKenzie's action-spy thriller The Fourth Protocol (1987), derived from a script by the original novelist Frederick Forsyth, featured Michael Caine as British intelligence agent John Preston and future James Bond Pierce Brosnan as Russian agent Maj. Valeri Petrofsky. In this mildly diverting film the KGB plans to destroy the NATO alliance by planting an agent (Brosnan) in Britain to assemble and detonate an atomic device. One of Britain's top spycatchers, Preston (Michael Caine), discovers details of the plan and races against time to stop it.

The late eighties era of Bond featuring Timothy Dalton was not without its influences. You can detect John Buchan, Hitchcock, Indiana Jones, Yojimbo, and Miami Vice in various places during the Dalton films. In the 1990s, Tom Clancy's techno-thriller novels became a movie series with numerous films featuring CIA agent Jack Ryan. Alec Baldwin played Ryan in John McTiernan's The Hunt for Red October (1990) and Harrison Ford for Patriot Games (1992) and Clear and Present Danger (1994). Ben Affleck took up the role in The Sum of All Fears (2002) and Chris Pine later played the character. Jack Ryan, a bit like Batman and 007, seems like a character who can survive different interpretations and be updated. Jack Ryan has never really become a tremendously beloved or iconic character though.

James Cameron's True Lies (1994) starred Arnold Schwarzenegger as Omega Sector secret agent Harry Tasker. The film doffs its cap to James Bond early on when Tasker emerges from a lake and removes his wetsuit to reveal a tuxedo underneath. When True Lies came out there was much speculation that the James Bond series was old-hat and the action-packed True Lies was the new order of things with its elaborate effects, nuclear explosion finale, and violence. As fun as True Lies was though, audiences were more than happy to see 007 back the next year and, on the plus side, he wasn't saddled with Tom Arnold as a comedy sidekick. True Lies seems a bit dated now with its slightly sexist subplot and Middle East villains but the action, as one might expect of James Cameron, is terrific. When Arnie activates his harrier jumpjet missile (with the villain hooked on it!) and says "You're fired!", well, that's a Bond quip if ever there was one. Sean Connery and Roger Moore would have delivered that line in style.

Despite the Charlie Higson novels there have been no Young Bond films yet but we've had If Looks Could Kill (aka Teen Agent) (1991) - the feature film debut of Richard Grieco, a teen-oriented spoof of the James Bond films. There was also Spy Kids series and Stormbreaker (based on the Alex Ryder

series of novels) and Agent Cody Banks (2003) plus its sequel
Agent Cody Banks 2: Destination London (2004). Spy Hard
(1996), a low-brow spy comedy, starred Leslie Nielsen as Dick
Steele (Agent WD-40) battling armless mad-man villain Andy
Griffith - who has plans to conquer the world. The film is
worth catching just for the Binderesque title sequence with
"Weird Al" Yankovic's Thunderball style song. Oh, and one
funny cantaloupe joke. Mike Myers' overrated Austin Powers
series spoofs the epic early Bonds, Derek Flint and the
swinging sixties in general.

Pierce Brosnan took over as Bond in 1995. Brosnan's Bond era
certainly had modern influences in a lot of its action - the Die
Hard franchise, John Woo, True Lies, The Matrix.
Interestingly, you could even argue that Tomorrow Never Dies
takes something from films like WarGames and Hackers with
its technological villain manipulating everything with a
keyboard. One could argue that the action sometimes became
quite generic in the Brosnan films with a shade too much
gunplay - something which mirrored current trends. In 1996
Geena Davis played an assassin for the CIA suffering from
amnesia in Renny Harlin's 'park your brain at the door and
enjoy' action epic The Long Kiss Goodnight. Shades of Kill Bill
and Jason Bourne, the film plays like a cross between James
Bond and Die Hard with a female lead.

Released in 1998, Ronin is an action/thriller that tells the
story of a group of former intelligence agents who team up to
steal a mysterious metal case. Starring Robert De Niro, Jean
Reno, Natascha McElhone, Stellan Skarsgård, and Sean Bean.
It is best known for its extensive and well staged car chase
scenes. 2001 brought us Spy Game, directed by Tony Scott,
and starring Robert Redford and Brad Pitt. The film focuses
on on veteran CIA operative Nathan Muir (Robert Redford),
whose protégé Tom Bishop (Brad Pitt) is scheduled for
execution in a Chinese prison. It's Muir's last day before
retiring, and Bishop is being deliberately sacrificed by oily CIA
officials to ensure healthy trade with China. Muir has 24 hours
to rescue Bishop. Brad Pitt turned down The Bourne Identity

to do Spy Game - thus paving the way for Matt Damon.

In 2001, computer game icon Lara Croft made it to the big-screen in Lara Croft: Tomb Raider. A female mixture of James Bond, Indiana Jones, Emma Peel and Bruce Wayne, the film wasn't a critical hit (though Angelina Jolie was praised in the title role) and only managed one sequel. Future James Bond Daniel Craig, with dodgy American accent, played the male lead. Lara Croft had her own gadget wizard in the spirit of Q - as did (a very Bondish) Bruce Wayne in Batman Begins and Hugh Jackman in Van Helsing.

XXX saw Vin Diesel as an American extreme sports champion railroaded into a James Bond ripoff film. Samuel L Jackson plays M and XXX even gets his own weapons expert, or Q as he's called elsewhere. As with True Lies there was much talk of how 007 had been beaten at his own game but XXX did not become much of a franchise. It had a terrible sequel (sans Vin Diesel) directed by Lee Tamahori. Vin Diesel later returned for the truly abysmal XXX: Return of Xander Cage. The avalanche sequence in the original XXX was a case of 'been there, done that, got the t-shirt' for the Bond series. And on the subject of action sequences, did the blue-screen freefall sequence in Arnie's Eraser remind anyone of Moonraker's PTS?

In 1996 Brian De Palma made a big-budget and complicated big-screen version of Mission: Impossible. Full of gadgets, locales, double-crosses and action, Tom Cruise starred as Agent Ethan Hunt. Hunt returned in more expensive glossy sequels with Bond style villains and beautiful women. Anthony Hopkins even turned up as an M type character and gave a glimpse of how great he would have been if given the part in the Bond series. On the subject of action sequences (again) did the sequence in the second film where Cruise and Thandie Newton bump cars around a dangerous mountain road in Mission: Impossible II remind anyone of the near identical sequence at the start of GoldenEye? The Mission Impossible franchise continues to go from strength to strength with the last three entries all excellent. Mission Impossible: Fallout had stunts the modern 007 films could only dream of.

In 2002 the first of three Transporter films starring Jason Statham arrived. Flashy and hollow but entertaining, these films were somewhat Bondish at times. Statham played a former special operations soldier who now earns a living 'transporting' valuable items in his car. The Transporter films were full of car chases, fights, and shoot outs. They were no threat to the Bond franchise but decent entertainment - if very much of their time.

The Bourne Identity is a 2002 action-thriller film based on Robert Ludlum's 1980 novel. It was directed by Doug Liman. The film begins with Italian fishermen rescuing a man who is floating inert in the Mediterranean Sea. The man turns out to be American but he is suffering from amnesia and has no idea who he is. A laser projector found upon him gives the number of a safe deposit box in Zürich so the amnesiac man decides to travel there and investigate. The safety deposit box reveals money in various currencies, numerous passports with different names, and a gun. He decides to take the passport bearing the name Jason Bourne. Our amnesiac hero is still pretty confused - although that safety deposit box probably should have tipped him off to the fact that he might be a spy!

Bourne enlists the help of a young woman named Marie Kreutz (Franka Potente) as he seeks to find out who he really is. It transpires that Bourne is a product of Treadstone - a black ops project intended to train and deploy elite assassins. This would explain why Bourne is a martial arts expert who can drive like James Hunt. Bourne's troubles have only just began though because Treadstone have become aware of his existence. Bourne had failed in an assassination attempt against exiled African dictator and Treadstone now plan to terminate him. To this end they activate a number of assassins to kill him.

The Bourne Identity (and its first sequel) were patently the biggest influences on the reboot of the James Bond series that arrived in 2006. Bourne is a very different character from Bond. He is not prone to quips and doesn't have much of a taste for the high life. He's a bit of a blank to be honest. James Bond is a loyal servant of Her Majesty (which will obviously have to be changed to HIS Majesty going forward) and a blunt instrument for his government. Bourne, by contrast, has no loyalty to the establishment and operates as a lone wolf. Bourne doesn't trust his own government - and for good reason because their covert agencies are usually trying to kill him.

The government spy racket is murky, corrupt, and dangerous in the Bourne films. The good thing about The Bourne Identity though is that it doesn't hammer you over the head with this theme. It simply uses this premise to deliver a satisfying and sleek action film. What really got the attention of EON was that The Bourne Identity cost $80 million less to make than Die Another Day but turned out to be a lot more exciting. Die Another Day has two gadget laden cars firing missiles at each other in a winter wonderland. The Bourne Identity on the other hand has Matt Damon driving a Mini Cooper through the streets of Europe being chased by the police. The car chase in The Bourne Identity cost considerably less money than the one in Die Another Day but guess which one of these car chases is the most fun? It's no competition. The car chase in Bourne is fantastic and has not a gadget in sight.

The Bourne Identity showed that you could strip away the CGI and outlandish trappings but still make a terrific spy thriller. The film also put us at the heart of the action much more than Bond movies had done of late with hand held-cameras and tightly shot fight scenes. The fight scenes in The Bourne Identity are enjoyably violent and superbly staged. They were a huge influence on the violent close quarter fights we got in Casino Royale.

Now, not to say that Bourne wasn't partly inspired by Bond in the first place. The Bond series hasn't been short of good tough fight scenes. Sean Connery's 007 had memorable scraps with

Red Grant and Peter Franks. Bond's fight with 006 in GoldenEye was pretty good too. The Bourne Identity also takes inspiration from classic Bond films in the way that Bourne has to use his wits to get out of dangerous and tricky situations. Bourne slowly being cornered from all sides at the Embassy is somewhat reminiscent of the way that Bond in OHMSS constantly finds himself surrounded by baddies in the snow frosted town just before Tracey turns up again.

One thing that helps The Bourne Identity too, and it is something which a lot of modern Bond seem to lack, is that Matt Damon has a nice believable sort of chemistry with his leading lady Franka Potente. Potente is obviously not supposed to be anything like a Bond Girl because Marie is just an ordinary bystander who ends up helping Bourne. Even so, The Bourne Identity shows that you don't need necessarily to cast the FHM model of the month as the female lead if you make a spy thriller.

The Bourne Identity is not as much fun as the very best Bond films of yesteryear and has quite a sullen, even bleak sort of atmosphere (humour is thin on the ground) but the locations are authentic and the action delivers. The music is terrific too. The emergence of the Bourne films was a double-edged sword as far as the Bond franchise goes. The Daniel Craig era used the influence of Bourne to its advantage with the success of Casino Royale but then to its disadvantage in Quantum of Solace.

In 2004, Jason Bourne returned for the sequel - The Bourne Supremacy. This turned out to be a very solid sequel. After the murder of Marie, Bourne heads back to Europe and is soon kicking ass in his usual efficient fashion. The main difference in this sequel is that Paul Greengrass replaced Doug Liman in the director's chair. Greengrass is notorious for his particular camera style. This is best described as shakycam. The screen wobbles around and we are put right in the centre of the action. The style of Greengrass works well in Bourne but to a point.

After a couple more films of this the obstreperous ADD camera antics of Greengrass got a bit tiresome and old. The Bourne Supremacy is fine though. The car chases are frenetic and the fight sequences pack a wallop. In 2004, The Bourne Supremacy still put the latest Bond films to shame when it comes to action. The success of The Bourne Supremacy was the catalyst for the preposterous editing style of Quantum of Solace. The lesson was simple. Bond benefits from some of the leaner, tougher action of Bourne but should definitely not try to copy the editing style of Paul Greengrass. It just doesn't suit Bond at all.

The fairly well received third film The Bourne Ultimatum arrived in 2007. The Bourne Ultimatum was more of the same really. Plenty of great action delivered through shakycam. By now EON were basking in the glow of the critical reception to their reboot Casino Royale. By hitching some of their wagon to Bourne they had managed to put Die Another Day behind them and steer the ocean liner that is the Bond franchise in a different direction. Quantum of Solace proved to be something of an iceberg but the ship's path was corrected again with Skyfall.

Jason Bourne was not really a character who could go on forever like Bond so it probably wasn't a surprise that the movie franchise fizzled out in the end. The Bourne Legacy was a fairly pointless spin-off without Matt Damon and then Damon and Greengrass returned for the 2016 film Jason Bourne. Jason Bourne showed that what was fresh and novel in 2002 wasn't fresh and novel in 2016. The shakycam, Matt Damon being all subdued and miserable, and murky government offices full of computers all now now seemed tedious in this uninspired sequel, By now though the Craig films were now influenced by a different franchise.

In 2005, Christopher Nolan began a new Batman series with Batman Begins. The film had Christian Bale as a very James Bondish Bruce Wayne and Morgan Freeman as Lucious Fox, an employee in a mysterious section of Wayne Enterprises who becomes an ally and is essentially Wayne's version of Q from the Bond films. Nolan's love of the Bond franchise is very evident in the gadget scenes. Nolan, a brave choice at the time for Batman Begins, puts Batman into a more real world than the Gothic/camp Batman films produced in the late eighties and early nineties and this effect is heightened by our fresh knowledge of how Batman came to be. The film has many striking images and makes good use of Scarecrow's mind-altering gas for some nightmarish effects. The climax is exciting and the relationship between Bruce Wayne and Alfred is deftly developed and touching.

It was really after the sequel The Dark Knight that the Bond franchise began to become noticeably influenced by Nolan's films. One could argue that Skyfall is heavily influenced by The Dark Knight - especially when it comes to the villain Silva. Heath Ledger won numerous plaudits for his Joker in The Dark Knight and he deserved all of them. The Joker of the comics was often aristocratic and erudite. Jack Nicholson's Joker, though great fun, was played for laughs. This Joker, Ledger's Joker, is just a force of nature. A mad bomber terrifying everyone in the city. Ledger's Joker is scary because we know he doesn't care about anything except chaos. He isn't motivated by money. Ledger is compelling, strange and funny as the iconic villain.

In the sequel, Morgan Freeman's Lucious Fox character supplies Wayne with a dazzling amount of cool gadgets and technology to use in various inventive ways. It's ironic really that the initial Craig Bond films ditched Q for being too silly whereas The Dark Knight - a sombre and well, dark, film - still uses the character in a clever way for its own ends. It is perhaps no coincidence that Mendes brought Q back for Skyfall after the Nolan Batman films emerged.

The Dark Knight also includes one of the best James Bond pre-credit sequences never made when Batman attempts to kidnap a Hong Kong criminal from a skyscraper and escape via a waiting plane. Mendes was influenced by this neon cityskape aura in Skyfall. Another obvious inspiration is that The Dark Knight is moody and sombre. It's a trifle pretentious if you are being honest. Moody, sombre, and slightly pretentious are all qualities you could apply to Skyfall.

One could argue too that No Time to Die takes some inspiration from The Dark Knight Rises in the way that both are exceptionally long and give a specific era of these respective heroes a definitive sort of ending. As we have noted though, the influences go both ways because Nolan is plainly putting a lot of James Bond influences into these films. The Bruce wayne/Lucious scenes in Batman begins in particular suggest that Christian Bale could have been a pretty good James Bond had he been cast back in the day.

The action film landscape in the latter part of the Craig years was dominated by Marvel and the Fast and Furious franchise. Marvel was an influence on the connected nature of the Bond films but you wouldn't say that the Fast and furious franchise (which is gleefully daft) has been a salient influence on the Craig era. The other action franchises in these years seem to owe as much to Bourne as Bond. The Liam Neeson film Taken is like a sort of Tesco Value version of Jason Bourne. The first Taken film is very watchable but the two sequels were very mediocre and forgettable.

The John Wick franchise with Keanu Reeves has also been popular. In these movies, Reeves plays a retired hitman who ends up on violent crusades which inevitably result in him killing millions of people. Wick is sort of like a neo-noir Jason Bourne. The neon mansion festooned nightclub world Wick inhabits though is often stylish and heightened and this aspect was most likely influenced by James Bond. The list of films and franchises the Bond series, over many decades, has had to keep pace with is endless and varied. No other franchise or action character though has been as enduring as James Bond. The Craig era then has been influenced by Jason Bourne, Nolan's Batman films, Mission Impossible and many others. Jason Bourne is the key influence though. There might not even have been a 2006 Bond reboot without the Bourne films.

The debut film of any Bond has an obvious advantage in that it is a novelty. We are watching someone completely new play James Bond for the first time - and that is always fascinating. Casino Royale suffered from a fair amount of media negativity (Bond fans are probably well aware of the CraigNotBond website and newspaper headlines like 'James Bland' and stories about Craig getting his teeth knocked out doing a stunt) during its production but in a way this actually worked to the film's advantage because it lowered expectations. Casino Royale turned out to be an efficient and well made film and Daniel Craig was well received too. The fact that Craig was so different to Pierce Brosnan also worked to his advantage. After the cartoonish mayhem of Die Another Day, Casino Royale felt like a breath of fresh to most fans and critics.

Casino Royale felt lean and tough and took a leaf (more of a forest really) from the Bourne series by making the fights more brutal. It was a well cast film too with some excellent actors. The film isn't perfect (my own attention tends to drift somewhat during the long poker section) and the last act is a trifle melodramatic at times but Casino Royale showed once again that Martin Campbell had an uncanny knack of refloating the Bond franchise in tricky circumstances. Casino Royale had a 'classic Bond' sort of feel that the other Craig Bond movies failed to recapture. The artistic merit of Casino Royale was a double-edged sword in many ways. EON now had to work out what to do next with Craig's Bond in the films which followed. As we've discussed, they somewhat struggled at times in this task.

EON eventually stumbled across the notion of making the Craig era connected. They tried to make it seem like they were telling one big epic story. As we have noted, this led to some clunky exposition at times. The Bond franchise is not Star Wars or Lord of the Rings. It doesn't really need too much connective tissue - even within a specific era. Take the Dalton era for example. You can watch The Living Daylights and

Licence to Kill in isolation or in any order. It doesn't really matter. Felix Leiter turns up again in Licence to Kill and is played by a different actor than portrayed him in Daylights. It isn't a huge issue though. We just accept these adventures on their own terms.

Imagine though if Timothy Dalton had come back in 1995 and his third film had been a sequel to Licence to kill. Bond is now retired and living with Pam. He finds out he has a child with Lupe. Blofeld is back and it turns out that Blofeld was the person who funded and manipulated all the villains in both Daylights and Licence to Kill. Bond is depressed and suicidal. He ends up sacrificing his life to save Lupe's child. That all sounds daft but then it's not a million miles away from where the Craig films ultimately ended up in terms of their approach in No Time to Die! The backstory and melodrama in the Craig films did threaten to overstay its welcome in the end.

It is best then to just accept that the Craig era is its own thing. The Craig era does not comfortably slide into the franchise as a whole and is, as far as Bond films go, atypical and even somewhat experimental. It was doubtless the modern fad for long form storytelling (both on television and in the Marvel movies) which led EON down this path. Would the Craig era, in artistic terms, have been any more or less successful if it had simply stuck to the stand alone 007 format of the past? That is impossible to say with any degree of certainty. We simply don't know.

Daniel Craig successfully accomplished the most important task of any Bond actor and any Bond era. That is simply to hand over the baton to the next iteration with the series still in fairly rude health. No Time to Die might not have hit the box-office heights which may have been possible in less troubled times but it still proved that there was a tremendous appetite for James Bond around the world. No Time to Die was a very big deal in 2021 and generated huge amounts of publicity and anticipation. You can expect Bond 26, when it finally arrives, to do the same. As for the future of Bond films, in terms of their approach and style, that is, at the time of writing, completely up in the air. We simply don't know what comes next and EON probably don't either.

In time though EON will finally begin to rumble into gear again. They will decide on which direction the next iteration of Bond will go. A million actors, both plausible and preposterous, will be alleged to be in contention to play Bond. Flavour of the month models and singers will be rumoured to be the female love interest. Exotic locations will be scouted. New gadgets invented. Scripts penned. Directors interviewed. A deluge of prospective theme songs will tumble forth. Commercial brands will be signed up. Stories about Bond's next car will emerge. Endless acclaimed thespians of varying nationalities will be mentioned as the next prospective villain. In the end it will all slowly fall into place again. A press conference will be arranged and Barbara Broccoli will finally reveal the actor who has replaced Daniel Craig. And then the familiar cycle of James Bond will begin all over again. A new era will commence. James Bond shall continue to be forever.